THE RURAL NEGRO

THE RURAL NEGRO

BY

CARTER GODWIN WOODSON

NEW YORK / RUSSELL & RUSSELL

REPRINTED FROM A COPY IN THE COLLECTIONS OF
THE BROOKLYN PUBLIC LIBRARY

FIRST PUBLISHED IN 1930 BY THE ASSOCIATION
FOR THE STUDY OF NEGRO LIFE AND HISTORY
REISSUED, 1969, BY RUSSELL & RUSSELL
A DIVISION OF ATHENEUM PUBLISHERS, INC.
BY ARRANGEMENT WITH THE ASSOCIATION
FOR THE STUDY OF NEGRO LIFE AND HISTORY, INC.
L. C. CATALOG CARD NO: 69-16771
PRINTED IN THE UNITED STATES OF AMERICA

To

ARCHIBALD HENRY GRIMKÉ
BY WHOSE NOBLE EXAMPLE OF HEROIC
EFFORT IN BEHALF OF AN UNDERPRIV-
ILEGED CLASS THE AUTHOR HAS BEEN
INSPIRED TO WRITE THESE PAGES

CONTENTS

ILLUSTRATIONS

TABLE, FIGURES AND DIAGRAMS

INTRODUCTION

This book is another by-product of the three-year survey of the social and economic conditions of the Negroes of the United States since the Civil War, a task undertaken by the Association for the Study of Negro Life and History in 1926. Inasmuch as most Negroes live in the South, this work bears mainly upon the status of these people in this particular section of the country. Confined to rural people, then, the book treats only of conditions obtaining among the peasants and persons living in centers of not more than two thousand five hundred inhabitants.

To develop this subject special investigation was required. Questionnaires were sent out, and thousands of them with data were returned and studied. This method, however, was not depended upon altogether. When filled out even in the presence of investigators in answer to queries propounded by them questionnaires do not always reveal the truth of a situation. Persons filling them out sometimes misunderstand the questions, and those who do grasp the meaning become conscious of being made objects of investigation and, therefore, give evasive answers. A considerable checking up, then, was found to be necessary.

The investigators of the Association used the questionnaires largely to find clews to things more important than what was generally disclosed. They went to the people's homes, approaching them indirectly as ordinary visitors, and after winning their confidence obtained facts which otherwise could not have been collected. In many cases these investigators collected written and printed materials to support what persons had to say about themselves and the communities in which they lived.

Such verification was necessary not only in the case of questionnaires but even in that of reports of the United States Bureau of the Census. The reports of one decade are seldom worked out on the basis of the one preceding or the following. One is, therefore, often in error in making comparisons. To know what has actually happened among Negroes considerable field work is an absolute necessity, and this has been the method followed in the development of this study —actual observation, personal knowledge, and documentary evidence.

This book is, therefore, documented only to the extent that its facts are drawn from sources other than the archives of the Association. Where no references are given it is understood that such facts are collected by this agency and are supported by data now on hand. This method has been deemed wiser than frequent citation of reports and the like which have not been made available by publication.

CARTER GODWIN WOODSON.

WASHINGTON, D. C.,
April, 1930.

THE RURAL NEGRO

THE RURAL NEGRO

CHAPTER I

KEEPING ALIVE IN THE COUNTRY

IT is often said that health is the greatest problem of life. No man is more useful than he is sound. Without good health he cannot undertake or carry out efficiently any of the difficult things of everyday life. With good health man finds it possible to outstrip disease in the struggle of life. Wise employers of labor, therefore, have long since learned to consider the housing, living conditions, and recreation facilities of their employees. The intelligent peasantry has been rapidly learning to do this for themselves as far as they have been able. In the rural districts where the Negro population is numerous in this country, however, such providence is not generally found. For this reason the death rate of the Negroes in some of these parts exceeds the birth rate; and the wiseacres have begun to predict that the Negro is on the way to extermination, when as a matter of fact experience has shown that adequate attention given to the health of these people will cause the pendulum to swing the other way.[1]

The main reason for giving such little attention to the health of the Negroes in the rural districts is

[1] Louis T. Dublin, Statistician of the Metropolitan Life Insurance Company, has well established this fact with data set forth in his *Health and Wealth.*

ignorance, among both the Negroes themselves within such areas and among persons outside of such areas. It was formerly thought that the health of man was well taken care of by nature itself when he lived in the country. It was said that he breathed pure air, ate fresh food, drank limpid water, and evaded the

"In Shameful Impudence"   Cabin with Mud Chimney

attacks of germs which make inroads on the health of people in urban communities. Most people of our day, however, have learned to question these assertions: but unfortunately the neglected Negroes in the rural communities have remained embalmed in their ignorance of the laws of health. They have not had sufficient education and contact to learn how to live.[1]

[1] Inasmuch as the rural whites are not much better informed than the Negroes there will be little hope for the latter until the former are enlightened.

In the first place, it is not true that the man in the rural community breathes pure air. The air in its purity may be there, but he may not always make use of it. While working in the open, as most laborers in the country must do, they get the benefit of the air in its all but perfect state. Because of ignorance of the laws of health, however, their lungs are too often

A Rural Home

impoverished by lack of ventilation. These peasants suffer thus because of the rather general custom of sleeping two or three together in the same bed and all with their heads under cover to make up for the lack of proper heating or insufficient blankets. It is a common thing for these people to keep the windows closed from the time air first becomes chilled in the fall until the coming of warmer weather the following year. The cracks and holes in the walls of their huts and the frequent use of the door are often their only salvation.[1]

In such ignorance it does not help the case when in better circumstances these people build ceiled or lathed and plastered homes to take the place of the log huts in the rural districts; for with such habits they are more fortunate in cabins where the air can find its way into the rooms through apertures in the walls. Statistics show also that these people from the country easily fall as victims to pulmonary troubles when they migrate to urban centers and live thus in modern homes. Physicians constantly report the difficulty of keeping these patients' windows open. These inadequately clad people cannot get rid of the idea that cold air is injurious to health while warm air is most conducive thereto.[2]

With respect to pure food the Negro in the country is far from being amply supplied. In the small farm districts of the upper South, where Negroes are independent farmers observing the need for a rotation of crops or working for small planters who do, the food supply is not much of a problem. Such farmers produce a large portion of the food they consume. However, in the sugar and cotton plantation districts, where the one crop idea has not yet been uprooted, the Negro tenants and laborers must live on such food as is supplied to them by the plantation commissary: and their inadequate income together with the terrorism in vogue makes it impossible for the majority of such persons to improve their daily fare. They buy the most unsatisfactory food and pay for

[1] Epstein, *The Negro Migrant in Pittsburgh; The Negro in Chicago*, 192.

[2] This statement is based upon information obtained from various physicians of the districts surveyed.

it the highest prices. The average man must live on rough corn bread cooked without lard, fried fat bacon or pork, salt fish, sorghum or molasses, hominy or rice occasionally, and coffee or tea along with sufficient sugar sometimes to make a little dessert. Most of these things, except in the sugar district, must be obtained elsewhere. The soil is rich enough to produce vegetables in abundance, but the time of the laborers is required in the production of cotton or sugar, and these things must be imported or foregone. If brought in, the best vegetables would never reach these peasants, for such eatables would find a much better market among persons more favorably circumstanced.[1] Rural Negroes, then, too often have a diet of which they may have quantity but lack vitamine power.

The water supply in such parts is often more of a problem than in the upper South. The alluvial plain does not give the water the same chance for purification which it has in the region of the artesian wells and flowing springs. Because of flood conditions and tendencies toward subtropical diseases in the lowlands of the cotton and sugar districts, too, the water as well as the air tends to be more easily contaminated than in the case of the section farther north. These peasants' habits of living, moreover, are such that they know little about filtered water and seem to care less; and even if they did know, their limited time and small income would often render its procurement impossible. Furthermore, as long as the water looks clear and does not have a

---

[1] Dealers in foodstuffs have certain classes of foods designated for wealthy districts and other sorts of eatables for parts inhabited by the poor.

disagreeable taste, the uneducated peasantry never think of it as being impure even when they see it frequently used as a home for insects and reptiles.

The attitude of these Negro peasants toward the much-talked-of germs, too, is not dissimilar. Among them such theories have just begun to have a hearing, and few of them have been converted to such doc-

AN OLD SLAVE HUT   A RURAL HOME WITH FLOWERS

trines. The houses are usually without screens, and the flies, mosquitoes, and other insects may have free access to the inner circle of the home. If these things, although dropping occasionally into the food, do not actually remain in it there is not much cause for worry. These people, moreover, have been thoroughly inured to the once troublesome bites of these pests. That they carry germs is known here and there, but the thought with them is still a theory. Most diseases result in the natural course of things, or they come as the vengeance of God to afflict the wicked. Of course, the "conjure doctor" there is still active. He plants "the snake powder and the rabbit foot," and when the victim for whom they are intended steps over them he "falls sick with an incurable disease or instantly drops dead." Only some other voodoo agent who is wise enough to discover the trick can bring relief, and he may come too late.[1]

Under such circumstances, then, there is little impediment to the spread of diseases except such as nature itself provides. A little precaution is taken in case of the smallpox or yellow fever scare, but few think seriously of the dangers of mumps, measles, scarlet fever, pneumonia, or tuberculosis. Gonorrhea and syphilis are often treated lightly as ordinary complaints; for unfortunately these peasants do not know the importance of thorough treatment of these maladies according to modern discoveries. The rage of these diseases in the rural districts is not so uncommon as people ordinarily believe when thinking of the cities as "the only centers of vice." While open prostitution is not practiced in most rural districts as in urban communities, there are sufficient moral lapses to spread venereal diseases. The situation becomes alarming among such unsuspecting people when an infected prostitute returns from a sojourn in cities to her native rural district after having been

[1] It is a mistake to think of such superstitious practices as originating in Africa. Investigation has shown that the Negroes have taken over so many of them from the whites that it is difficult to draw the line between European and African influences. See the preface of Puckett's *Folk Beliefs of the Southern Negro* et passim.

deceived in thinking that "stolen waters are sweet and bread eaten in secret is pleasant."

One would naturally inquire here into the public health service to find out what the state is doing to prolong the lives of these people. With respect to the Negroes in the remote districts, it may be said that the public is doing practically nothing. Health at public expense is almost as slow a development as education at public expense. For centuries many

A NEGRO HOSPITAL AT SUMMERVILLE, SOUTH CAROLINA

persons opposed the tax on property of citizens to educate the youth; and, so far as the Negro is concerned, certain parts of the United States still maintain this position. The people as a majority to-day, in the area of the dense Negro population, are still indifferent about the health of any of its citizens. They are yet unable to understand that a country with a healthy people is naturally more prosperous than one of a diseased population. With respect to the Negroes there is still more lethargy. Vitiating race prejudice precludes the possibility of their getting as much consideration as the members of the other race; and for some reason there seems to be an un-expressed belief that the Negroes can survive with less provision for their health than other members of the human family.[1]

The average reader will be inclined to think that this picture is overdrawn. He knows of the vital statistics kept by his city or county within the regis-tration area, the constant attention directed to the death rates of cities, and the efforts made through State departments of health and the departments of physical education of the schools. Almost every city or town has something to say or to do about health. In 1926, too, thirty-three States had laws regarding the teaching of health and physical education in their public schools. Fourteen of these States had ap-pointed directors of health and physical education, and most of the State departments of education had made definite requirements regarding the training of teachers for this work.[2]

It must be remembered, however, that this health work is a recent awakening, and the whole effort has not yet been reduced to a practical basis. The au-thorities are still undecided as to what their objec-tives should be. They differ as to what health education is, whether it should be taught in the public schools, why the health of a child is a responsibility of the school administration, and what a complete

[1] Because people in enlightened parts have long since learned better the layman is too apt to think that such advancement is general. The observations of five investigators in various rural communities support this position.

[2] The information was compiled from various reports of depart-ments of health, local, state and national.

health program is. Sex education with a view to
teaching morals, moreover, has been a much mooted
question; and the exact time when such education
should begin is still another. The most perplexing
of all problems, too, is the question as to how much
of the public funds may or should be diverted to
such a purpose, or whether other needs are not more
urgent.[1]

NEGRO HOSPITAL AT OKMULGEE, OKLAHOMA

Then when comes the question of further taxing
the public, already burdened with a dual system for
the education of the races separately, the health of
the Negro must go lacking. In the first place, the
Negro rural teachers as a rule are underpaid, and,
therefore, unprepared for their tasks. Those fortunate enough to obtain an education secure better
positions in cities and towns. Negro rural schools,

[1] In some of the States moneys appropriated for one purpose have
been used for another, especially when a decidedly political machinery
happens to be in charge and can find some technical reason for such
action.

then, in such inefficient hands, can never carry out an intelligent health program. The lack of supervision by well trained directors employed in such numbers as to give attention to these remote districts presents another problem. At present the health program is being carried out largely in cities and towns in the well organized schools. Some teachers in rural schools do not see a supervisor of any sort

DELIVERING TO A NEGRO HOSPITAL A PATIENT WHO HAS JUST BEEN OPERATED ON AND BROUGHT THROUGH THE STREETS IN AN AMBULANCE FROM A WHITE HOSPITAL WHERE THE OPERATION WAS PERFORMED

more than once or twice a year. In many of the most backward districts such visits are not more frequent than one every two or three years: and even then the teacher receives practically no helpful suggestions as to how to improve his work; for unfortunately the supervising authority sometimes does not know as much about the task in hand as the uninformed teacher.[1]

[1] See below the chapter on rural schools.

Here and there, however, one finds an awakening. A few counties, as in the cases of Florida and North Carolina, have nurses to teach health to the people in the rural districts. The same thought elsewhere is now being carried by a few rural teachers to the pupils and their parents. Such efforts are so recent, however, that the people have not yet had time to heed such preachments as anything more than theories which these persons are paid to advance. Furthermore, the funds which local districts have been induced to appropriate for public health are so meager and the workers touching the rural districts are so few that, having so many to instruct, they have not achieved much. There has been such an unusual amount of talk in praise of the few efforts made that the uninformed public has thought of such uplift as general. Such laudatory comments have been justified on the ground that if you praise the public for what little it is doing it may be encouraged thereby to do more.[1]

Carrying out such a health program among Negroes has been hindered, too, by the lack of hospital facilities. In the remote districts there are practically no hospitals for these unfortunate people. There are only one hundred and eighty-three Negro hospitals altogether and a few white institutions which provide a number of beds for persons of color. Sixteen of the one hundred and twenty visited by Dr. A. B. Jackson in 1928 were of A grade, forty-three of grade B, thirty of grade C, twenty-seven of grade D or unworthy of support, four not entitled to the name; and in some cases conditions were so disheartening

---

[1] This method has often been followed by Negroes soliciting money for private schools.

as to justify abolition. Of these Negro hospitals only seven have been approved for internship by the National Hospital and National Medical Association, and of the one hundred or more Negro Medical students completing their courses each year only about thirty or thirty-five can secure internships. Since there are only one hundred and eighty-three Negro hospitals with a total bed space of sixty-five hundred,

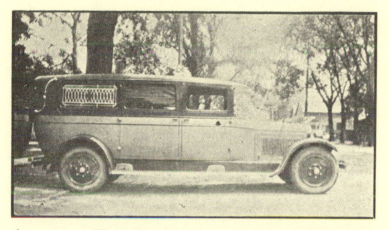

AMBULANCE IN WHICH NEGRO PATIENTS ARE BROUGHT FROM A WHITE HOSPITAL TO AN INADEQUATELY EQUIPPED NEGRO HOSPITAL AFTER AN OPERATION IN THE WHITE HOSPITAL

or an average of one bed for each two thousand Negroes, the situation has not much chance for improvement. Every white patient has fourteen times as good a chance for hospitalization as the Negro. In the case of tuberculosis the Negro has only one chance out of twenty-five. The death rate of the Negro, then, is remarkably low when we consider these handicaps. It is little wonder that it is not more than two to one.[1]

[1] These facts were obtained from the report of Dr. A. B. Jackson, who in 1928 made a survey of Negro hospitals for the National Medical Association and the National Hospital Association.

The general public is not interested in the extension of hospital service, and the rustic people themselves are too backward to appreciate the use of hospitals. Among the Negroes and poor whites hospitals are unpopular. Many of them have never seen such institutions and, therefore, retain the notion that they are still poorly equipped asylums kept like the almshouses of old. When these peasants hear that a patient has been sent to such a place they abandon all hope for his recovery and proceed to pray for the repose of his soul. Hospitals among these people, then, must come as a slow development both as a result of their poverty and their ignorance which makes the superimposition of the system a necessity. The high mortality of the patients treated at the nearby inadequately equipped hospitals has not permitted a rapid change in this all but medieval attitude.

Some few rural patients who may have sympathetic employers may have the opportunity of being carried to a distant hospital for treatment. Inasmuch as up-to-date hospitals for Negroes, even in cities are rarities, as indicated above, this trip may involve transportation to a place a hundred or two hundred miles away, and the patient may die en route. The writer recalls a case of a Negro section hand who was injured on the Chesapeake and Ohio Railway track a number of miles up in the mountains from Huntington, West Virginia. Friends rushed him on the train to the city of Huntington to the hospital of this very company in the service of which he had been injured. The patient, in a dying condition, was refused because this hospital was reserved for whites, and while his friends were going from place to place in the city to find some physician to treat him in a

private office, the unfortunate bled to death.[1] This
happened some years ago before West Virginia had
directed as much attention as it has since then to the
health and education of Negroes. Recently in Min-
neapolis, however, a Negro woman, carried to the
Thomas Hospital critically ill, was permitted to remain in her agony and to die while the authorities

A BABY CLINIC IN THE COUNTRY

were debating the advisability of receiving her. Another case of this sort was similarly handled recently
and resulted in the death of a Negro patient lying
at the door of a hospital in Wilmington, Delaware.[2]

There naturally arises here the question as to the
whereabouts of the country physician and his effi-

[1] The writer himself was living in Huntington, West Virginia,
when this happened.

[2] *The Crisis*, January, 1928.

ciency to cope with this rustic situation. Negro physicians are inadequate to the demand among their people. There is one such physician for about every thirty-three hundred Negroes whereas the whites have a physician for about every five hundred.[1] The profession is undermanned to the extent that few Negro physicians extend their practice far into the outlying rural districts, and a still smaller number live beyond the limits of cities and towns. The Negroes in the rural districts are not able to pay for modern medical treatment; and even, if they were, the prejudice against Negro physicians is often such that it is uncomfortable for them to dwell there.[2] The Negroes in the remote districts, then, are dependent upon such ministrations as the casual visits or calls for resident white physicians or visiting Negro practitioners will permit. Inasmuch as most of those rural blacks are found in that section of the country where race prejudice is most acute, the disinclination or the refusal of white physicians to attend promptly patients in dire distress may result in serious loss of life.

Knowing this to be the case, Negroes in the rural districts depend upon home remedies as much as possible. They understand the therapeutic uses of such as castor oil, salts, calomel, quinine, paregoric, and laudanum. They frequently fall back also on the use of watermelon seed tea, the concoction made from sheep dung, sassafras, and home-made bitters pro-

---

[1] Some of these white physicians would not be needed if they did not practice on Negroes.

[2] Negro physicians are sometimes driven away from the South for practicing on whites. White women and men with venereal diseases prefer the attention of a Negro physician, but the public does not always approve it. Dr. Roscoe Wilson had to leave Marion, S. C., on this account. Others, however, do well in this practice on white men and white women.

duced from herbs.   In such a case as childbirth, pre-
natal care is almost unknown, and a physician may
not be called at all.   The midwife often has complete
charge.   Sometimes, too, when a physician is available, these people, thinking that they know much more
about medicine than a trained advisor, fail to call for

"How to Care for the Diseased Chickens"

professional assistance until it is too late.   When they
are so fortunate as to make the proper diagnosis,
however, speedy relief is often effected by hot applications and other home remedies.   Friends and relatives must try their hand at the cure before they
give up and appeal to the physician as the last resort;
and even when the physician is attending the patient
they may *kill* the sufferer with their interference with
other applications.   The physician's position, then,
is the most difficult one of not only curing the sick,

but of making at least the pretense of all but raising
the loved one from the dead.[1]

Unfortunately, too, the country physician is generally inefficient. Unless the people upon whom he
practices are much better off than the average rural
folk, the practice does not afford sufficient income to
attract a man who is well qualified. The best-trained
practitioners naturally go to those urban communities where they receive most for their services. They
leave the unproductive rural districts for those backward, elderly men who have not kept pace with the
profession, or for young men who may engage in
practice in rural communities merely for the experience or because they cannot find an opening in a more
profitable field. The older men know little about the
up-to-date methods of treating diseases and the modern methods of preventive medicine. Both they and
the younger men in the rustic situation, moreover,
have not usually the equipment or hospital facilities
for practicing what they may actually know. About
as far as they go when visiting a patient is to inquire
into his living habits, listen to the account of his
complaint, look at his tongue, feel his pulse, and leave
the stereotyped prescription which may kill just as
easily as it may cure. Under these circumstances,
then, it is remarkable that so many of these people
have lived.

The Negroes so unfortunately situated must die.
Figures show that the death rate in the registration
area was 18.2 per cent in 1925; 17.6 per cent in 1924;
and 17.7 per cent in 1923. This was 48 per cent
higher than the white rate in 1924 and 62.5 per cent

---

[1] Numbers of physicians who were interviewed gave this as one of
the causes of a rather high death rate.

higher than in 1925, while the Negro death rate is higher in the cities than in rural districts, being 23.5 per cent and 15.2 per cent, respectively, in 1925. The rural death rate of Negroes in the South, however, was 14.8 per cent whereas in the North it was 23.4 per cent. In 1925 it was shown that while the death rate a thousand population for rural whites was 10.84 per cent, that of the Negroes was 16.13 per cent.[1]

Many diseased Negroes who happen to survive show all sorts of deformities. Bow-legs due to lack of proper care in infancy; protruding teeth resulting from the failure to remove the milk teeth at the proper time; imperfect hearing due to lack of attention in serious sickness; and failing vision arising from unnecessary strain of the eyes. Other deformities result from inherited diseases coming like afflictions of sinful fathers visited unto the third and fourth generations. Society has stood aloof and said it cannot be prevented. In this particular group, many say, there is a predisposition to die prematurely, and the only thing possible is to await the solution of the problem by time. A little hope has been seen, however, in the awakening to the fact that germs developed in the neglected Negro element of our population do not draw the color line, and while they take their toll of those in whom the majority of public functionaries may not be interested they carry off also those whom they deeply regret to see pass away. The reason for unusual precaution in the prevention of diseases, then, has been thoroughly convincing to the public; but the public conscience has not yet been adequately quickened to construct a working pro-

---

[1] Dublin, *Health and Wealth*.

gram to include all or even the large majority of these people in the backwoods districts.

To meet these needs one finds here and there various suggestions to improve the health of the Negro peasantry. The extension of hospital service, of course, is desirable, and there is a chance for a more general use of those already available in cities inasmuch as the improved roads make the transportation easier. There is some effort to increase the number

A VIRGINIA FARMER'S HOME

of county nurses, but only in North Carolina has this idea been actually translated into a program action. Philanthropists have thought of establishing health centers from which nurses and physicians may operate as their base very much as the rural teachers do in the schools. The Julius Rosenwald Fund, long interested in the Negro, has appropriated a sum to provide for thus extending such medical attention to Negroes. It is hoped that the Negroes themselves

will become alive to the situation, and that the public
will give its support in working toward an efficient
health program to which this philanthropy points.
Here, as in other cases, the Negroes who have given
their centuries of service to enrich others are unable
to provide for themselves the ordinary facilities of
health. Those whom they have faithfully served are
being entreated to come to their rescue and in so
doing free the whole nation from the fetters of ill
health and disease.

CHAPTER II

THE majority of Negroes, or sixty per cent of them, live in the country. The life of the people thus situated gives a key to the understanding of most of the group; for, while the urban Negroes are increasing in importance, the rural Negroes are still the larger factor. How these persons make their living, then, is an important question in the study of this element of our population. At first approach, however, the question seems to be a simple one. Most persons living in the country till the soil for a subsistence. There is not much else to occupy the peasants except so far as a few others may be engaged in ministering to the special wants of the tillers of the soil. In this special class serving the agricultural group, moreover, the Negroes do not always figure as conspicuously as the whites.

Yet even in the treatment of agriculture here as the main concern of the rustic group of Negroes one would make a mistake in dismissing it as a question already answered or self-explanatory. We are accustomed to reduce things to the average of a class and to generalize with respect to the whole group; and when we have finished we may have met the demands of the casual observer, but we may be far away from the truth from the point of view of one seeking definite information. The Negro in this country, rural or urban, is so situated that everywhere he is an exception to the rule whether we believe it or not. In the rural districts where one would least expect such conditions to obtain there is little deviation therefrom.

Of the many questions arising here a few must be noted. The Negroes in the rural districts belong mainly to the farming population, but what element of that population do the Negroes constitute? The

T. M. CAMPBELL, FIELD AGENT OF THE UNITED STATES DEPARTMENT OF AGRICULTURE, PRESENTED WITH SOME OF HIS MANY FRIENDS

Negroes thus employed have been characterized in so many ways that it requires investigation to learn the truth. Are the rural Negroes independent planters, tenants, or farm hands? Are those toiling in the fields laborers for wages or bondmen? Are the Negro tenants really such indeed or peons in violation of the Thirteenth Amendment? Are the Negroes playing the part of an important factor in agriculture, or are they merely being used as a means to an end?

After all, is there much better chance for the Negroes to make progress in the rural communities than in the city? Does the appeal to the Negroes to return to the country come as an invitation to improve their condition or an urgent request from landlords who would like to exploit them just as they are now being exploited by captains of industry in urban centers? On which side of the shoe is there the more pinching?

These questions arise here because the recent tendency of Negroes to concentrate in industrial centers, where competition with white laborers has resulted in racial antagonism and bloody race conflict, has caused the districts embarrassed by this exodus to sing beautifully of the happy state of the Negro peasant who has remained in his lowly cabin and diligently served his landlord in the agricultural districts. The city is regarded as the burying ground of the Negro ill adapted to urban life. He has, therefore, been urged to remain on the farm. To contrast here the advantages of the urban Negroes in the North with those of the rural Negroes in the South is not a part of our task. It is sufficient to say that while some refer to the exercise of civic rights, better facilities of education, higher wages, and helpful contact with men and things of worth, the advocates of the rural life for the Negroes in the South warn the migrants of unemployment, poor housing, congestion, race riots, and the ravages of pulmonary diseases. They emphasize at the same time the ease with which one can earn a living in Southern rural communities. Negro leaders themselves, too, from the time of Frederick Douglass up to the present, have urged Negroes to forego the desire to seek their fortunes in the West or North and remain in the South where in large numbers they will figure eventually much more effectively in the affairs of the nation than they will when scattered throughout other sections. The fact that in spite of such preachments the Negroes have continued to leave the agricultural sections of the South is evidence of the unfavorable conditions obtaining on the farms. People do not easily migrate on account of

THE MAN BEHIND THE PLOW

persecution or religious or political differences. These things may be contributing factors. When people rise in large numbers to leave their homes for permanent abodes elsewhere, it is usually because they can make a better living where they are going than they can now where they have been residing.[1]

[1] The migration of the Negroes from the South has been discussed in Woodson's *Century of Negro Migration*, Donald's *Negro Migration of 1916-1918;* and Scott's *Migration of the Negro during the World War.*

To understand the Negro farmers, however, we must subject the class to an analysis. In the first place, let us note the various classifications of farmers as reported by the United States Bureau of the Census. At the top of the list come farm owners: those operating their own land only and those operating in addition to their own land some land rented from others. Then come farm managers who operate

THE TRACTOR AND THE NEW DAY

farms for their owners for wages. Finally there are the tenants constituting five classes. These will be mentioned in detail in the following chapter.

The relative numbers of farmers will be interesting in giving this picture. In 1910 there were 218,972 Negro farm owners and 218,612 in 1920. In 1925 there were 194,540 colored farmers in the South alone not including managers and tenants. Negro farm ownership lost between 1910 and 1920 but decreased

TABLE I.—FARMERS, BY COLOR AND TENURE

ITEM (See definitions in Introduction)		The South	Geographic Divisions		
			South Atlantic	East South Central	West South Central
Number of Farmers, by Color and Tenure, 1925					
Total	White	2,299,963	782,003	725,225	792,735
	Colored	831,455	326,058	280,827	224,570
Full owners	White	1,173,778	471,040	398,213	304,525
	Colored	159,651	78,941	38,928	41,782
Part owners	White	150,875	41,095	51,403	58,377
	Colored	34,889	18,228	9,281	7,380
Managers	White	10,259	5,720	1,607	2,932
	Colored	667	417	124	126
Tenants	White	965,051	264,148	274,002	426,901
	Colored	636,248	228,472	232,494	175,282
Cash tenants	White	103,854	36,230	34,614	33,010
	Colored	78,760	25,841	44,231	8,688
Croppers	White	278,736	90,643	90,230	97,863
	Colored	344,322	119,767	128,147	96,408
Other tenants	White	582,461	137,275	149,158	296,028
	Colored	213,166	82,864	60,116	70,186
FARMS OPERATED BY CROPPERS					
All land in farms, 1925—acres		22,985,660	8,550,314	6,071,743	8,363,603
Crop land harvested, 1924—acres		16,093,431	5,166,635	4,548,734	6,378,062
Value of land and buildings, 1925—dollars		1,133,205,380	370,446,922	287,143,445	475,615,013
Value of implements and machinery, 1925—dollars		39,871,615	12,520,417	9,980,133	17,371,065

in the South between 1920 and 1925. In 1910 there were 1,544 farm managers, and 2,226 managers in 1920. In 1910 there were 678,118 tenants and 714,441 in 1920. Thus tenancy increased between 1910 and 1920 but apparently decreased between 1920 and 1925. Comparing these statistics with those for the white farmers we see that there were 3,707,501 farm owners in 1910 and 3,691,868 in 1920. In 1910 there were 56,560 farm managers among the whites and 66,223 in 1920. In 1910 they had 1,676,558 tenants and 1,740,363 in 1920. Thus it would appear that while the whites decreased a little in farm owners from 1910 to 1920 they increased in farm managers and tenants. Yet the loss in farm owners is not proportionally as great as that of the Negro farmers. For several reasons the Negro farmers have found it easier to make a living elsewhere, and they have been leaving the farms. Only the share tenants who are more disadvantageously situated have tended to remain on the farms and to increase.

Yet when we consider the size of the farms owned by Negroes in comparison with the size of those owned by whites we get a still better view of the disadvantage of the Negro farmer. In 1920 the farms operated by white owners averaged 168 acres; by white tenants 136.3 acres; and by white managers 810.2 acres. Farms operated by colored owners averaged 71.6 acres; by colored tenants 38.9 acres and by colored managers 213.7 acres.[1]

Eighty-six per cent of the farms reported as being operated by white owners, moreover, were under full ownership and fourteen per cent part ownership. In

---

[1] *Colored* here means that in this calculation the enumerators of the Census Bureau included the few Japanese, Chinese and Indian farmers.

the case of the colored farmers the figures were eighty-two and a half per cent full owners and seventeen and a half per cent part owners. Yet, as the United States Census report indicates "the land in the farms of the white part owners in 1920 amounted to more than one-fourth of the total land farmed by white owners, the average size of these part owned farms being more than twice that of the farms

A HOME IN THE COTTON FIELD

operated by white full owners. Among the colored farmers, on the other hand, the average size of farms operated by part owners was less than that of farms operated by full owners."[1]

[1] Tenancy statistics show other differences. The most disadvantageously situated tenants are those operating on the share basis. To this class most of the Negro tenants belong. Of the farms operated by tenants under the forms of tenancy mentioned above 69.1 per cent of the white tenants operated their farms on a share basis, 23.8 per cent on a cash basis, and 7.1 per cent on a share-cash basis; while 72.8

The size of the farms of colored farmers in the
South compared with that of the white throws further
light on the question. The farms of the white owners
in the South averaged 149.7 acres in size in 1920, with

per cent of the colored tenants operated their farms on a share basis,
26 per cent on a cash basis, and 1.2 per cent on a share-cash basis. It
is clear then that while the proportion of colored tenants operating on
the cash basis is slightly higher than that of the whites, the colored
have a larger number operating on the share basis and very few on the
share-cash basis. Inasmuch as the report for 1910 showed 64.6 per
cent of the whole number of white tenants were operating on shares
while 57.2 per cent of the colored thus operated, that cash tenants
represented 28.2 per cent of the white and 40.5 per cent of the colored
tenants, there was an increase of share tenants during that period and
a corresponding decrease of cash tenants, the change being most marked
in the case of the colored farmers. Other figures from the accompanying table show that while the percentage of farms operated by
tenants has increased during the preceding twenty years for both
white and colored farmers, white farmers showed the greater increase
for the decade 1900 to 1910 and colored farmers the greater increase
for the decade 1910 to 1920.

The South shows a much larger proportion of colored tenants than
whites. Only 38.9 per cent of the white farmers were tenants in 1920
while 76.2 per cent of the colored farmers were tenants at that time.
The undesirable condition of the colored farmers is further shown by
comparison with respect to the relation to their landlords. For example, standing renters, those who pay a fixed quantity of the product
for the use of land, were reported in 1920 as being 27,072 white
tenants and 77,929 colored. In the case of the croppers, that is,
tenants over whom the landlord exercises more control because of
furnishing work stock, the colored showed 333,713, while the number
reported as share tenants proper was 176,711. The colored croppers,
those in this dependent relation, then, were nearly twice the number
of the regular share tenants, or 47.4 of all the colored tenants in the
South. At the same time only 227,378 whites were classified as
croppers and 474,513 as share tenants, the number of white croppers,
therefore, being less than one-half as great as the number of regular
share tenants and constituting only 25.6 per cent of all white tenants
in the South. The croppers condition becomes worse, as is often the
case, when they are operating under the plantation system of manage-
ment, the plantation being divided into small tracts which are operated
by the tenants under very close supervision. The best way to appreciate the tremendous number of persons thus affected is to bear in
mind that only about one-fifth of the farms occupied by Negroes are
actually owned by them. The others are rented. The Agricultural
Census of 1925 does not indicate much change for the better.

59.7 acres improved, as compared with an average size of 64.7 acres and 33.3 acres improved for colored owners. The farms of the white tenants averaged 90.4 acres in size, with 49.2 acres improved, as compared with 38.2 and 28.9 acres respectively for the total and improved acreage of farms operated by colored tenants.

The value of the land thus operated, too, will

PICKING COTTON

further illuminate the situation. Reporting on the total value of farm property such as land, buildings, implements, machinery, and live stock on farms operated by whites in 1920, 69.5 per cent was returned for farms operated by owners, 33.4 per cent for farms operated by tenants, and 4.1 per cent for farms operated by hired managers. In the case of the colored farmers the corresponding figures were 27 per cent for the owners, 71.6 per cent for tenants, and 1.4 per cent for managers. The distribution of the value of farm property among the several tenure classes of both white and colored, according to the census report, followed very closely the distribution of improved land in farms. For both white and colored farmers the figures for 1920 show a smaller percentage of the total value for owners and a larger percentage for tenants than in 1910. In the case of the ownership of live stock in the South the difference

How to Make Better Hay

is very pronounced, especially since work animals, horses and mules, constituted 63.1 per cent of the value of all live stock on the farms of colored operators in 1920 but only 42.2 per cent of the value of all live stock on the farms of white operators.[1] White farmers are introducing machinery more rapidly than the colored.

[1] *Negro population in the United States, 1790 to 1915*, pp. 559 to 564; and *United States Census of Agriculture, 1925*, pp. 14 and 15.

While the size of the farms, the distribution of improved and unimproved land, however, must be carefully considered in this comparison, we shall find ourselves far away from understanding the status of the Negro farmer unless we know something about the sort of land he owns. We must consider its productivity, its location with respect to the flood or tide, and the facilities for transportation. To say that

LOOKING AFTER HIS CATTLE

the Negroes of a certain county have as much or more land than the whites would not necessarily imply that the Negro farmers are wealthy in that proportion. Land is not uniformly fertile, and even should it be known that a certain acreage owned by Negroes is as fertile as that owned by whites in the same area that would not be evidence of equal wealth unless other contributing factors showed the same equality. Unfortunately, throughout the rural districts where Negroes are found in large numbers these other conditions are usually so unfavorable that the Negro farmers find themselves too handicapped to make much material progress.

In the first place, most of the land owned by Negroes is the land which poverty stricken whites have had to abandon to engage in something more lucrative in urban centers, or it is the land which the white farmers have worn out and abandoned as unproductive. In getting rid of some land which they had in excess of what they could find labor to cultivate, too, others have disposed of the least productive. There are, of course, some cases of Negroes who have acquired the estates of their former masters. Such instances are more frequent in the upper South, in the undulating or hill districts where the plantations were not large. In the cotton and sugar producing sections of the South, however, the old plantations have been kept mainly in the hands of the whites even when they are broken up in smaller parcels. This accounts for the large number of Negro tenants in that section. The lands there are not generally for sale, and even if they were the Negroes cannot easily save sufficient money to purchase this high-priced land regarded as the most productive of the whole South.

This keeping of the old plantations intact, however, has been exaggerated by writers who have done no more than to show how difficult it has been to deviate far from the system in vogue before the Civil War.[1] A much larger number of plantations have been broken up or parceled out than some writers would have us believe, but this does not mean that in the partition of them Negroes always become their

[1] *The American Historical Review*, XXX, 738-753; and *The Georgia Historical Quarterly*, XI, 254.

purchasers. Some of these plantations have been purchased by rich Western and Northern men who have used them for reserves or who have introduced farming methods different from those formerly applied. Such newcomers are found in considerable numbers in the border states, especially in Northern Virginia. They are beginning to go farther South and especially into Florida. This, of course, reduces

A LESSON IN HORTICULTURE

the chances for the Negroes to get hold of such land.

In the hill district of the upper South where the acquisition of land by Negroes has been a little easier the Negroes even there have not come into possession of the best land. The alluvial plains along the streams and the fertile soil of the tidewater section are both still owned largely by the whites. The Negroes, as a rule, must buy the rocky or swampy land far removed from town, from the railroads, or from the navigable

streams. The advantage must always go to the landlord disposing of the land unless misfortune over-
takes him and compels him to get rid of it all. This
is not so often the case, and even when such a thing
happens, there are usually well-to-do whites who are
in much better position to purchase desirable land
than the hard working Negro peasants. In only a few
cases has the South permitted the mulatto children
of white planters to come into the possession of the
estates of their parents. Southern courts have usually decided against such just heirs unless settlement
is made prior to the death of the planters thus disposed.

A considerable number, almost a fourth of the Negro farm owners, then, being unable to make a living
on such land as they own, must rent additional ground.
Not a few of such Negro owners have merely a small
parcel of land to raise a few vegetables and fruits
required by the family while the staple from which
the additional income is made is produced on rented
land. Such farmers naturally have a basis for more
independent action than the poor Negro who has no
land at all, but if the parcel of land of the owner
happens to be unusually small he may be just as
dependent upon the landlord as the laborer or tenant
who lives in one of the plantation cabins. The whole
family, wife and children, may have to go out daily
to work on the land of the large planter, abandoning
altogether the small farm except to give it such attention as a little chopping in the early morning, late
in the evenings or on holidays, when not required to
direct their attention to the major concern.

The Negro farmer could do a little more with his
present possessions if he had more capital or credit.

He can easily buy the necessities of life up to the extent of his earning power, but this in the rustic seats often presents an opportunity for what the business world calls "fleecing." The Negro buys at the highest prices and sells his crop at the lowest. If he had a little capital with which to purchase his supplies for the year at wholesale rates and to hold

A DEMONSTRATION TO IMPROVE CULTIVATION

the crop until the value of his product increased, his story might be different from his tale of usual woe; but, starting out with the disadvantage of borrowing to plant his crop, he is compelled to continue it throughout the year. His margin, then, is so small that he does little more than to help the middle man to increase his wealth at the expense of the peasant.

There has been much talk of advancing money to poor farmers at low interest and for a long period to make the planting economical and their marketing profitable; but these loan facilities have been used largely by those who already enjoy the advantage of having some capital and can qualify as borrowers from the financial institutions, which would hardly think of granting such opportunities to the class of poor farmers to which most Negro owners belong. No money is loaned except to farm owners in possession of land appraised by the agents of the farm

A COUNTRY BOYS' CLUB

loan banks as having considerable value. So far as lending money to them is concerned they are rather the victims of the policy that "to him that hath it shall be given, and from him that hath not shall be taken away even that which he hath." The white planters and country merchants are the borrowers from financial institutions, and they are thereby enabled to extend credit to the Negro peasants whom they economically control.

What is herein said, however, does not mean that

a few Negro farmers have not wonderfully improved
unproductive or worn-out lands disposed of to them.
Being industrious and without the handicap of the
white man who regards labor as undignified, the
Negro farmer with the aid of his wife and children
has often made such unproductive areas apparently
blossom like a rose. With less capital he has been
able to accomplish proportionately more than his
aristocratic white neighbor; but this seemingly favorable aspect is not altogether encouraging. If the
industry of the poor Negro peasant enabled him to
do so much more than the unprofitable white farmer
how much more could this Negro have accomplished
had he been as favorably circumstanced as his white
neighbor, and how much more wealth he would have
produced not only to enrich himself but his country.
After all, a man has but so much energy to spend
in this life. If he has to work always against handicaps he must finally fall short of his possibilities, and
the country which thus hampers him for the apparent
benefit of the privileged class is hanging a mill stone
about its neck. Such a country eventually must fail
in competition with those which have no such im-
pediments.

Along with agriculture goes personal and domestic
services as the employment of a considerable number
of Negroes in rural communities. The large majority
of Negroes thus engaged, however, are in urban centers. Yet the planter must have some one to cook,
clean, wash, and iron; and in the case of wealth there
may be need for expert tailoring and personal attendance. This is a part of the program in the pro-
motion of agriculture. As such labor is regarded by
the whites as undignified, just as working in the

fields is so considered, the Negroes have a monopoly of such positions. The Negroes thus employed, however, have had little chance for enlightenment and their service is not always satisfactory. Apparently, then, the Negroes in menial positions have retrograded, for they were once praised because of their efficient service. The fact is, however, that the better

A LESSON IN RAISING PIGS

class of Negroes once restricted to these lower pursuits have advanced higher in the sphere of labor or they have developed independently enterprises of their own.

Persons formerly thought that Negroes trained along practical lines in the industrial schools would enter such service, but such workers seldom penetrate the rural districts to earn a livelihood; and statistics show that most Negro graduates in domestic science

and art do not serve the whites. The majority of
them operate independent establishments in towns or
restrict their efforts to their own circles. There has
been some talk and some effort has been made to sup-
plant the untrained and inefficient Negro domestics
with whites from the East, but the employers know
that they cannot deal as despotically with white laborers as with Negroes, and white employees of other

IMPROVING THE BREED OF SHEEP

parts do not find inviting the conditions of the rural
South. Increasing the efficiency of domestic servants
in rural communities, then, has been as difficult as
improving agriculture.

To solve some of the problems of the Negro
farmers the extension departments of the industrial
schools and the fourteen Land Grant Colleges have
done much to teach the Negro farmer how to make
the most of his situation. Agricultural education has

been carried to the people. Instructors, inspired by
Booker T. Washington, have taught the farmers the
chemistry of the soil, rotation of crops, scientific
fertilization, drainage, and conservation. How to
husband their present resources and to develop along
with their farming such as stockraising, poultry, and
dairying, have also been demonstrated so as to open

SHOWING FARMERS HOW TO SHARPEN TOOLS

to these peasants new possibilities. The very home
life of certain parts has been elevated, too, by the
women extension workers who have taught house-
keepers plain sewing, sanitary cookery, the preservation of food—in short, how to live on what they
ordinarily throw away.

Into a few liberal sections these workers have carried the ideas of coöperative buying and selling.
With this, however, they have not gone very far for

the reason that it is difficult to bring together a group
large enough to compete with the gigantic corpora-
tions in their tremendously large transactions.   In
selling, too, the Negro farmers thus coöperating suffer
from the undependable handling of their produce
which, unless rushed, will perish before it gets to
market; and even then the freight rates are so high
that in case of a distant city from one-half to two-
thirds of the amount received for the produce has
to be paid for transportation.[1]

Some improvement of the situation, too, has resulted from the tendency of the Negroes to leave the
impoverished districts when they are allowed freedom
of action.   While some land has been abandoned,
those farms left in operation have been able to secure
better prices for staples produced in smaller quanti-
ties.   The decline of those sections suffering from the
migration to urban centers, moreover, has caused
the large planters and the lending class to see the
necessity for granting the Negro farmers more consideration to make them content to remain in agriculture where they are needed.   Some few centers of the
abandoned districts have actually organized commit-
tees and sent out workers to preach the gospel of
good will and interest in the uplift of the poor Negro
farmers.   The lure of the city, however, especially
since others returning from such centers have reported the many facilities for earning a livelihood,
has tended to drain off these farmers to industrial
establishments where they may be temporarily in
demand, but where they often suffer terribly from un-

[1] This statement is based upon data of these associations examined
by investigators.

employment after they have burned their bridges behind them.

This farming area, however, has not suffered so much from the migration as some have said, and for that reason certain parts have granted Negroes less consideration than is generally reported. In fact, some communities have told the Negroes to go. The mechanization which has recently taken place in the industrial world has eliminated the necessity for much farm labor, and at the same time it has increased crops while decreasing the acreage. The machines can produce more than could be done with work animals and at the same time rendered the cultivation of a large acreage for food for such animals unnecessary. The South is, therefore, producing just as large crops as formerly and doing it with less labor. There is no scarcity of labor at present in the agricultural area, according to official reports of 1929 of the United States Department of Agriculture. The Negroes returning from the industrial centers to the South to-day are not coming back always to the place where they are urgently needed.

CHAPTER III

TENANCY

IN spite of improvements here and there, agriculture in the South is handicapped by the peculiar turn which it took immediately after the Civil War when a readjustment in the economic system became necessary. Nominal slavery at least had passed away, but the dependence of the poor freedmen upon their former masters remained to continue the institution in another form. It was naturally expected that the planters would adopt the wage system of paying the laborer a definite amount in money for his service by the day, month, or year; and as a matter of fact some of these landlords did so, as was and is the custom among most of the farmers of other sections of the country. In the majority of cases in the area devastated by the sectional conflict, however, the owners of large plantations thought that their interest could be better taken care of in their impecunious condition by adopting a system which has become known as "tenancy." The freedmen had little choice in the matter. They were dependents who had to take whatever was offered them or drift into vagabondage.[1]

History has shown, however, that although there might have been some good intentions which prompted land owners in this direction, it has proved to be the

[1] This has been discussed in *The Journal of Negro History*, IX, 241-364, 381-569; XI, 243-415, 425-537.

worst evil from which the South has to suffer. Thinking people who can see future consequences from an error of the past and present commonly refer to "tenancy" as an evil much worse than illiteracy, intemperance, or lynching, about which we daily hear so much from the rostrum and the press. In fact, "tenancy" is in a large measure the cause of these other evils in the South. The system has given rise to a transitory, migratory class which has no perma-

A HOME AT REMLEY'S POINT, SOUTH CAROLINA

nent attachment to and no abiding interest in the communities in which they sojourn. "Tenancy" supplants the idea of home ownership, and thus prevents the building of a desirable rural civilization as is the case with absentee ownership. The agencies like the school and church under such circumstances cannot carry out any constructive program where there is no permanent home life. This class of mentally and spiritually undeveloped people, then, whether whites or blacks, necessarily show evidences of evil habits, irreligion, and lawlessness.

What then is tenancy? Ordinarily we refer to tenants as persons paying for the use of property, but otherwise just as independent in their transactions as the owners of the property themselves. In the case of farm operators in the South, however, the significance is more far reaching. In the first place, there are many different kinds of tenants, each one enjoying more or less independence or exercising more or less liberty in proportion as he finds himself closer to or farther removed from the owner of the land. The persons thus occupied are generally spoken of as tenants, renters, or croppers. All of these operate only rented land. Yet for a better understanding of their situation the United States Bureau of the Census divides them into five classes: share tenants who pay a certain share of the crop for the use of the land but furnish their work animals; croppers whose work animals are furnished by the planters; share-cash tenants who pay the rent partly in cash and partly in products; cash tenants who pay cash altogether for the use of the land; and standing renters who pay a stated amount of farm products for the use of the farm land.[1] The croppers and standing renters are the most dependent of all classes of tenants. Almost everything is furnished them by the owners of the land, and consequently they receive less of the returns from their labor. Being so dependent, they are allowed such a little liberty that their will is subject almost altogether to that of the landlords to whom they are attached.

These relations are usually determined by conference with the tenants about the beginning or end of the year. They agree then to sign a contract which

---

[1] *Negro Population in the United States, 1790 to 1915*, pp. 459 to 464; and *United States Census of Agriculture*, 1925, pp. 14 and 15.

may be enforced at law. Inasmuch as these illiterate people have little or no knowledge of law, they sign away their own rights and liberties, not knowing what they are doing. Most of these contracts are decidedly unfavorable to the tenant, but in addition to this disadvantage the interpretation of the agreement is altogether in the hands of the planter assisted by the

ONE OF THE MANY HOMES IN THE RURAL DISTRICT

officers of the law whom he can always summon to his assistance and make the contract mean whatever he desires it to be. So far as the Negro tenants are concerned they have no law to which they can appeal. For them law is the will of the particular planter with whom they may be dealing. To question his word or to invoke aid against the carrying out of his wishes would be a disastrous procedure for the tenants. A tenant, therefore, easily becomes a peon or slave, about whose condition we shall hear in the next chapter.

This low status is well reflected in the contracts very much like the following lease which tenants have had to sign:

Said tenant further agrees that if he violates the contract, or neglects, or abandons or fails (or in the owner's judgment violates this contract or fails) to properly work or cultivate the land early or at proper times, or in case he should become physically or legally incapacitated from working said lands or should die during the term of his lease, or fails to gather or save the crops when made, or fails to pay the rents or advances made by the owner, when due, then in case of full possession of said premises, crops and improvements, in which event this contract may become void and cancelled at the owner's option, and all indebtedness by the tenant for advances or rent shall at once become due and payable to the owner who may treat them as due and payable without further notice to the tenant; and the tenant hereby agrees to surrender the quiet and peaceable possession of said premises to the owner at said time, in which event the owner is hereby authorized to transfer, sell or dispose of all property thereon the tenant has any interest in, and in order to entitle the owner to do so, it shall not be necessary to give any notice of any failure or violation of this contract by the tenant, the execution of this lease being sufficient notice of defalcation on the part of the tenant, and shall be so construed between the parties hereto, any law, usage or custom to the contrary notwithstanding.[1]

The routine of the work of these laborers will enable us better to understand the status of these tenants. After the cropper has agreed to become a tenant he

[1] American Statistical Association, *Quarterly Publications*, XIII, pp. 82 to 83.

comes under the supervision of the landlord who
sends out his rider, a man employed to supervise all
work on the plantation. This white boss apportions
the acreage for cultivation, decides the amount of
fertilizer each family must use on its parcel of land,
when the crop should be planted, and on what particular spot. The cropper is obligated to rise as early
as there is sufficient light to work, about four o'clock

A NEGLECTED HOME

on long summer days, and he must toil until dark.
There is a bell or some other signal informing the
croppers when to start and when they may stop work.
If his wife and children work in the fields, either she
or some nearly grown girl is permitted to stop about
eleven to prepare dinner. On some plantations the
dinner intermission is two hours on very hot days;
but on others only one hour can be spared. If the
planter happens to be liberal he allows the cropper

and his associates to cease work on Saturday afternoons.[1]

When the crop is harvested by the tenant the planter deducts therefrom his stipulated share and takes out also the value of clothing, food, and supplies which the planter has furnished the cropper during the year. If there is anything left the planter usually buys the cropper's residue, for the latter is not in a position to hold the crop for a better price, and few planters would permit such an exercise of foresight or business acumen even if the cropper so desired to do so.

Throughout the year both the landlord and the cropper have each tried to give the least and get the most out of an impossible situation. Inasmuch as the landlord has the advantage of owning the stock, the implements, the land, and sometimes by an unwritten law the cropper himself, the landlord usually has whatever apparent profit results from the transaction. Sometimes, however, the landlord sees that he is not making any headway at such an unprofitable task, and he disposes of the land to Negroes. In this way there has been some increase in the number of Negro farmers. This, however, does not happen so often as exploiters of philanthropists would have the public believe.

The extent to which tenancy exists in the South, therefore, will be further enlightening as to the Negro's condition in that section. In the South there are about 40,000 plantations with an average of about five tenants each. The history of tenancy, however, shows that with respect to the Negro it is slowly decreasing,

[1] For a general discussion of these advantages and disadvantages see "The Rural Life of the South," by John Lee Coulter in the *South Atlantic Quarterly*, XII, pp. 60-71; and American Statistical Association, *Quarterly Publications*, XIII, pp. 45-58.

although it still has a strong foothold in most of the
Lower South. Tenancy on the strictly renting basis
which obtains largely in the North and West is its
first step toward the breakup of large land estates and
the development of the small farming class. A large
planter has more land than he can properly cultivate,
and he rents out a part of it. If he finds this unprofitable he sells it. Farms in this country, there-

In the Center, a Typical African Woman on a Sea Island off
the Coast of South Carolina, Not Much Influenced by
Modern Culture

fore, have decreased in size; but at the same time they
have increased in number, although farm land has
increased very little since the Civil War. In some
parts the farmers have brought a larger acreage under
cultivation, but this may mean either one of two
things, an increase in owners or an increase in tenants.
Often, too, an increase in tenants means an increase
of the share croppers who are only one stage removed
from the wage hands. Almost half, more than one-
third of Negro farmers, are share tenants. A small

farming class is most desirable, but if the land tenure leads to a condition of the dependency of the tenant upon the landlord, which approaches serfdom, it becomes undesirable.

This is just what has happened in the South. While some plantations have been apparently divided into small farms operated by renters, they are hardly

AN OPPRESSED FAMILY   A WORKER IN GEORGIA

more than debased hired laborers whose plans of work are drawn up altogether by the owners of the land or managers employed by them. This was the fatal mistake in the economic reconstruction of the Southern States. More than half of the states of the Lower South have their farms thus worked and between 25 and 40 per cent of those in other parts of the South adhere to the same plan. Hardly one-third of the farmers in the Southern States employ labor. They prefer to buy it.

The present status is most nearly presented by the statistics of 1925.[1] According to this data there had been a slight decrease in tenancy but not enough to show any appreciable change in the status of the Negroes on the plantations. In 1910 there were 678,118 tenants; 714,441 in 1920; and 636,248 in the South alone in 1925. Other tenants of color are included in the figure for 1925 as in the cases of 1910 and 1920; and the 1925 report does not give the number of Negro farmers outside of the South. In 1925 these tenants were divided as 78,760 cash tenants, 344,322 croppers, and 213,166 other tenants. All croppers of both races operated 22,985,660 acres in 1925 and harvested 16,093,431 acres in 1924. The value of the land thus operated in 1925 was $1,133,205,380 and the implements used were considered as worth $39,-871,615.

This shows the large area of the soil of the South on which are stationed thousands of operators who have not much more of a future than that of slaves. Persons have included this area and these values in estimates to show what progress Negroes have made. That the Negroes are thus situated is no fault of theirs, but the fact is one for lamentation rather than a cause for the rejoicing so frequently indulged in by misinformants of the public. It may require a stronger force than those now operative to disrupt the present system and hasten the dawn of a new day. Practically all of the plantations which have broken up into small farms have done so because of being hard pressed or because the owner found farm-

[1] *United States Census of Agriculture*, 1925.

ing unprofitable. Few have been moved by the doctrine of the desirability of the small farming class.[1]

In view of these things some have advocated the breakup of the plantation. In defence of the system against peasant proprietorship, however, there have been advanced various theories. It is said that the small farm cannot be operated as economically as a large plantation. The small investment and the work

COTTON ON UNPRODUCTIVE SOIL

required would not permit an outlay for improved machinery, the introduction of the best stock, and the scientific preservation of dairy products, foods, and vegetables. As a matter of fact, however, the large planter does not always introduce modern appliances as soon as they appear. Industrial history shows that the large employer usually holds wages down to have his work done as long as he can by cheap labor to obviate the necessity for the outlay involved

[1] W. M. Brewer, *The Plantation in the Georgia Historical Quarterly*, XI, 254.

in the introduction of modern machinery. Experience has shown, moreover, that what the small farmer loses in being unable to practice economies of the large plantation the small farmer gains by coöperation with his fellows. If properly conducted, coöperative associations among the peasant proprietors may enable them to produce their staple just as economically

A COTTON SCENE ON A PROSPEROUS PLANTATION

as the large planters. The efforts of the agents of the United States Department of Agriculture and of the State Departments of Agriculture, assisted by workers from Land Grant Colleges and privately endowed industrial schools like Hampton and Tuskegee, have shown how this can be done wherever a sufficiently large number of such farmers can be induced to support community efforts of this sort. Such agents, however, are sometimes opposed by the planters because their efforts are considered prejudicial to the interests of the landed aristocracy.[1]

Investigators assert, too, that the rise of the small farm will be impossible as long as there is the absence of the instinct of land ownership. American native whites have become so accustomed to the abundance of free land that they do not generally aspire to ownership so rapidly as foreigners, who, coming from a country where land is scarce, quickly acquire it here. Only about a fourth of the Negro farmers are actual owners, but, as stated above, they are acquiring land much faster than the native whites. In the passing of the free arable land of the West and the concentration of people in cities requiring larger food supplies, land ownership is becoming more of an attraction and the idea is taking root in the tenancy area in the South. With respect to the Negroes, however, there are some whites who do not encourage their becoming owners of land and actually refuse to sell it to them. Some of those who believe that the Negroes should become owners, moreover, would restrict them to certain areas, carrying out the iniquitous principle of segregation which is now being worked out in cities. Here, then, is a social problem which the unwisdom of Americans has permitted to interfere with the solution of an economic problem which is doing so much to hold the rural South back.

Others advocate the hired labor system as the easiest solution of the problem of tenancy. Pay the laborer, they say, a fixed stipend, and then assume full supervision of his work. Every phase of the work

[1] This was the report of John McKinley from South Carolina from several places where this obtained; also that of a worker still active in Louisiana. The writer himself learned of such conditions in the backward parts of Florida and Alabama, which he surveyed.

could be so directed as to make it an harmonious operation. The whole plantation would then be developed according to the program of the planter only. This would make it much easier to introduce the latest farming methods, to rotate crops, introduce machinery, and fertilize the soil. The hired labor system would do just as much to increase production, to improve the breed of stocks and products, to increase the income of the owners, and to enhance the value of

COTTON PICKERS AT THE CLOSE OF THE DAY

the land. Under this system, too, the laborers would have ample opportunity to learn scientific farming.

The whole system would be educational, the laborer learning from the employer. Such hired laborers would learn to save sufficient money to improve their situation by becoming owners themselves. The principles of frugality and foresight not found in the shifting tenants would develop in the hired laborers. The hired laborers might first use their savings to become long time lessees and with the income accruing from their efforts they might purchase the very land which they rent. Production throughout the agricultural area would be systematized and agricultural resources would be preserved. The whole country would profit by this economic readjustment of a large producing area of the modern world.

To cure the evils of tenancy one finds here and there those who advocate long time leases as the first step toward peasant proprietorship. It is believed that both lords and tenants can be more easily induced

COTTON PICKERS "WEIGHING IN," AT HEMEMANN, SOUTH CAROLINA

to try out such a plan than they could be prevailed upon to dispose of the large plantations to small farmers. In support of this proposal its advocates argue that long time leases will change the attitude of the tenants toward the land which they cultivate. Instead of trying to get the most out of it by putting the least into it, they will cultivate the soil better, keep up its fertility, improve the buildings, devote some time to shrubbery and gardening, repair the country roads, manifest interest in education, and promote religion. Long time lease tenants will also show interest in coöperative organizations for the common good, pay more promptly their obligations to the local merchant or banker, invest their surplus capital in local enterprises, all of which will build up rather than bleed the community. In the case of long time leases, too, it is said that the relation between the landlord and the tenant will improve. The principles of equity and justice will prevail in their transactions. The long lease tenant will have more with which to buy land and become an independent farmer when he ceases to spend money annually moving from place to place seeking a better opportunity which he never finds.

The large plantation and tenant system are still with us, however, and good fortune resulting from the prevalence of the small farm, then, never reaches this area. The system prevents a diffusion of population by keeping permanently settled families far apart. This interferes with transportation because there are not sufficient progressive farmers along the way to build and repair roads and the large farmers may not construct them except for their own convenience. In such a scattered state telephones are not extended to the area, and if found there the connection is more expensive because of the few subscribers. A little contact means little diffusion of new ideas and a consequent running behind the forces of progress. Tenant farmers in such a situation do not know what is going on in their particular sphere and even if they did they would not have sufficient knowledge to make use of advanced information.

And shifting is what makes the situation worse. As most tenants toil from year to year without seeing any material change in their status or one cubit added unto their economic stature, they easily migrate. Hoping to better their miserable condition, they move from one plantation to another at the close of their contracts at the end of the year. According to the statistics of the United States Government nearly half of the Southern tenants move each year. If this tenancy could be rendered stable, the operators remaining on the same land from year to year, there would be less disaster in the system, but up to the

RURAL TEACHERS AT BRINKLEY, ARKANSAS, IN THE AGRICULTURAL AREA

present the problem has remained a troublesome one. The aspect of the areas thus afflicted, then, is that of worn out land, short crops, bad roads, rotten bridges, weather beaten houses, and littered yards.

It is almost impossible, also, to interest this landless, homeless, illiterate class in other forces for the common good of the country, so deeply implanted is selfishness or shortsightedness. To make the country attractive there must be labor saving devices, comfortable homes, modern schools, and live churches.

The tenant class of people will never demand these things; and, if superimposed, it will be difficult to extract the cost from the returns of these victims. Philanthropy which has been active in other spheres is just beginning to manifest interest in these things.

The reformer, however, meets with obstacles in promoting the various schemes of coöperation which have meant so much in the development of other rural areas. Tenants do not easily take an interest in coöperative stores, warehouses, creameries, cheese factories, marketing societies, purchasing societies, and breeding associations which have remade other rural communities in transforming the people into thrifty, progressive, and intelligent citizenry. Shifting tenants do not stay in one place long enough so to become acquainted with other neighbors as to learn to coöperate in such a serious effort as the business partnership which these measures imply. And even when such efforts are attempted in a modified manner in the light of conditions obtaining, the results have usually been too meager to warrant the outlay in time and energy. Tenancy, then, is the case of a man dying by his own hands and by his own error, brought on by a hardened sense or seared conscience which makes him believe that the cause is remote when it is within.[1]

People thus situated never advance far in education. Their children do not attend school regularly. They leave one school before they have reached proper grading and pass on to another where they do not stay long enough to be readjusted. In thus moving from place to place they lose what they have acquired from year to year; and, therefore, do not reach any

[1] Most of these views are advanced in the *South Atlantic Quarterly*, in Volume XII, pp. 60-71.

definite stage of mental development. In the absence
of a properly graded school system in the South
where the teachers are underpaid and consequently
inefficient, too, the schools under the most favorable
circumstances would not avail much in the uplift of
these people. As there is no compulsory school law
enforced among Negroes in these parts, the children

A LESSON IN SHEEP RAISING

of these peasants leave school as soon as they are
able to do work on the farms. Illiteracy among them
runs rather high, and those who obtain some smat-
tering of education can seldom do more than read
and write incorrectly.

The rural church suffers also in the same way from
the evils of tenancy. The pastor must face a new
congregation each year. If he has started with a
program requiring time for execution he must aban-

don it or try it out anew before he has had a chance
to put it to a test on those who have gone like birds
of passage after tarrying only twelve months. It likewise becomes increasingly difficult to keep up the
interest of the shifting tenants in serious matters like
things of the spirit. As they have no fixed abode they

GATHERING FROM THE GARDEN

restrict their interest largely to the immediate necessities of life.

The preacher to such a class, too, is not the best
prepared of his group. Only an intelligent man of
the greatest spirit of sacrifice could be expected to
spend his life in such an uninviting field. Those ministers who are not wanted elsewhere drift into this
service; and it becomes worse when the landlord
builds the church and actually chooses the minister
for the Negroes. Only the preacher who knows how

to safeguard the interests of the planter is allowed to function in the premises His sermons are censored, and if he is found saying or doing anything that might cause dissatisfaction with things as they are, he will have to leave forthwith and anon.[1]

The banker, the merchant, and the professional man suffer from tenancy along with the teacher and preacher. Credit extended this class may mean ruin to the business man. The tenant has nothing but his labor to sell, and if that is peripatetic the lender is left in a precarious position. To make up for such losses money must be loaned at a rather high rate of interest and goods must be sold at high prices to squeeze out of the honest tenants the amount necessary to make up for the loss of the few who are not honest enough to take care of their obligations promptly. Most of such tenants, however, have credit only in the commissaries of their landlords, and they dare not purchase their necessities elsewhere. In case of professional services rendered the creditor has a better chance when his fees are collected through the landlord; but here again comes the double cost in that the landlord must increase the amount sufficiently to reimburse him against any loss he may sustain in assuming such a responsibility.

The whole system, then, suffers from an unsuccessful effort to hedge in persons and force them to do what they are supposed to do, and at the same time it afflicts the unoffending class with the burdens resulting from the failings of others. The procession

---

[1] This statement is based on facts obtained by several field workers on the staff making this survey. In several places in Louisiana and Mississippi the planters or their representatives were found listening through the windows of churches to find out what Negro ministers said to their congregations.

along the circuitous route has begun, however, and must go on although a few see the error of their ways. But what does a knowledge of these things avail since one element in the equation cannot be eliminated without loss to all? When one moves all must go in the same direction. To stop the procession would be tantamount to a revolution, for it would destroy the present economic system at an apparent loss to all concerned.

That this condition of tenancy obtains is not to the discredit of the Negro, and he must not be misunderstood in the discussion of these undesirable conditions. The Negro has tended to rise from tenancy to ownership in spite of the difficulties involved. Negro farmers in the first place have been increasing at a faster rate than white farmers. This increase, too, has been not only in farms operated but in those actually owned. While the white rural population tended to be drawn off to the industrial plants in the South a generation ago, the Negro tended to remain on the farms. This obtained until the upheaval of the World War which carried the Negroes also from the rural communities to the cities. This migration, however, has gradually stabilized itself.

CHAPTER IV

PEONAGE

TENANCY, too, manifested in its most undesirable form, gives rise to a concomitant evil generally referred to as peonage. As pointed out above the most difficult problem of the tenant area is to keep the tenants on the land. The migration of shiftless tenants from one plantation to another is the problem of the problems. Unless the tenants can be kept on the land and can be made to take some interest in its upkeep the system of agriculture based on tenancy must fail. To solve this problem the landlords of some of these plantations have resorted to force upheld by the law. This, however, was not a new idea. Immediately after the emancipation of the Negroes in 1865 the devastated States hoped to secure labor by vagrancy laws which compelled every freedman to enter the service of some one and to remain therein for such wages as the ruling classes agreed among themselves to pay. Those freedmen who continued to loiter thereafter were arrested, condemned, and put to work on the public highways or leased to planters.[1]

Inasmuch as this was a return to actual slavery the Federal Government interfered and reconstructed these States on the basis of free manhood suffrage

---

[1] *The Journal of Negro History*, IX, 280-293; and XI, 250-272.

which prevented the return of involuntary servitude. Upon the withdrawal of the United States troops from that area in 1876, however, the Negroes were disfranchised and eliminated from the political sphere and the return to the overlordship of the planters was made easier. Although the Thirteenth Amendment and other legislation in 1867 made peonage

A Peon   Another Victim

illegal and unconstitutional, Alabama, Florida, Georgia, Mississippi, North Carolina, and South Carolina enacted a generation later evasive laws which provided for involuntary servitude for debt, and the courts of these States upheld such legislation.

This, of course, was not legalizing slavery as such, but from Mexico the planters had learned how to hedge around the letter of the constitution and laws of the United States by measures which compelled the employee to remain in the service of his employer. This was peonage. It was a form of involuntary servitude which prevailed extensively in Yucatan and especially in the Vallé Nacional where cheap labor was required in the cultivation of tobacco. The beginning of peonage in Mexico, however, has been traced as far back as the conquest by the Spaniards. Early in the history of that country the conquerors worked out a scheme by which the poor, especially the Indians, could be forced to do the work of the planters and mine operators; but it later became restricted in its meaning to those laborers who were compelled to serve their creditors to pay debts which by agreement they had pledged themselves to discharge in labor. The States referred to above, following this example, actually adopted this very system and enforced it in their rural courts. These laws penalized the failure to comply with contracts for employment, the enticement of laborers from their employers, the violation of a contract with a surety who had paid the fine of a misdemeanant, infractions of acts of vagrancy, and the operations of emigrant agents.[1]

Peonage developed as a most natural consequence of things in the agricultural South. The large planters constitute a borrowing class. It is customary for financial institutions to advance for a year sufficient money to cover the expenses of the landlord and his tenants, the amount being determined on the basis of one tenant for each twenty acres. The landlord, then, must hold his tenants by fair or foul means. If they desert him he is bankrupt. Authority, therefore, must

---

[1] L. M. Hershaw, *Peonage*, one of the *Occasional Papers* of the American Negro Academy.

be maintained with overseers using whips and guns to strike terror to the tenants who are kept down in the most debased condition. Negro women are prostituted to the white "owners" and drivers; and children are permitted to grow up in ignorance with no preparation for anything but licentiousness and crime.

The best example of peonage was furnished by the case of *Bailey* vs. the *State of Alabama,* in which the State law was declared unconstitutional by the

A POOR FAMILY ON A FARM IN SOUTH CAROLINA

United States Supreme Court in 1911. This law provided that any person who made a contract in writing to perform a service for another and thereby obtained money or other personal property from such person with attempt to defraud the person, and who left his services without performing that service or refunding the money or property should be guilty of a misdemeanor. The law further provided that any person who made a contract in writing for the rent of land and obtained money or personal property from the landlord with the intention of deceiving him and left

without performing such service, refunding the
money, or paying for the property, should also be
guilty of a misdemeanor. The penalty for the offense
was a fine not exceeding $300 and, in default of pay-
ment, imprisonment for a period of not more than
twelve months. To make this law further effective it
was amended so as to make the failure of any person
who entered such a contract to perform the service

A FAMILY NEAR ELBERTON, GEORGIA

or to cultivate the land or refund the money or restore
the goods, prima facie evidence of the intent to injure
his landlord or to defraud him. In the decision de-
livered by the Alabama Supreme Court, the accused
persons should not be allowed to testify as to his
intent or purpose or "to rebut a statutory presump-
tion."[1] Inasmuch as employers thereafter made such
contracts with their laborers, when only the employer

[1] 211 U. S., 452; and 219 U. S., 219.

and the employee were present, it became an easy
matter to enforce compliance with such contracts
through minor rural courts.

"The general way of securing victims," said one
investigator, "is for the employer or his agent to
proceed to some town or city and to hire a lot of
laborers, agreeing to pay them certain wages and
their railroad fare to the place of labor, and to advance them provisions from the company store, or as
it is commonly called the 'commissary.' The laborers
arrive and at the outset are indebted to the employer,
who sees that they trade out their wages at the commissary, and in many instances, by a system of de-
ductions and false entries, manages to keep the laborer perpetually in debt. If the laborer has a family,
so much the better for the employer; they must live
out of the commissary and if the laborer runs away
his family are detained at the camp. To enforce the
payment of such debts young children have been withheld from their parents. If the victim escapes the
law is invoked. He is arrested under false pretenses,
cheating, swindling, and false promises. There is
usually no actual trial. The arresting officer in collusion with the planter induces the victim to return
to work rather than go to jail," and "so he returns
to bondage with a heavier load of debt to carry, for
the cost of pursuit and arrest is charged to him. Often
no process is issued for arrest, but the employer ar-
rests without process, returns the prisoner to his
labor camp and inflicts severe chastisement. Many
of the labor contracts contain provisions to the effect
that the laborer consents to allow himself to be locked
in a stockade at night and at any other time when the

employer sees fit to do thus.''[1] A case of South Carolina is cited in evidence to show that the contract
provided not only for locking up in the stockade but
for such punishment as the employer saw fit to inflict.[2]

Peonage, then, was defined thus by a judge: ''It is
where a man in consideration of an advance or debt
or contract, says, 'Here, take me, I will give you
dominion over my person and liberty, and you can
work me against my will hereafter, and force me by
imprisonment, or threats of duress to work for you
until that debt or obligation is paid.' '' Experience
has shown, too, that the judge might have added,
''Until I, the planter, shall say that the debt has been
paid.''

The planter keeps the books and no Negro would
dare dispute his word as to the record; and even if he
did the minor rural court in collusion with the planter
would give injustice rather than justice should he
make such an appeal for his liberty. At the end of
the time the employer is usually smart enough to have
the employee sign some other contract by which his
labor will be bartered away for another year. In case
of a fine it is much easier to discover some other
charge which the local justice of the peace or constable would consider justifiable for keeping the peon
in his employ for additional time.

Peonage in its worst form, then, developed in the
chain gang. The unusual prosperity of the country
and, of course, of the South, necessitated a large labor
force. To supply this need it became customary
to fall back on convict labor. The first step in such
peonage was the ''benevolent'' practice of the white

1 *The Nation*, Vol. 82, p. 379.
2 This instance was reported as being published in the *Atlanta Constitution* in 1901.

men who would volunteer to pay the fines of Negroes convicted of minor crimes, and thus get them out of

WORKING WITH THE HOE

jail. The next step was to assure, by physical restraint, the working out of the debts thus incurred. Finally came the coöperation of justices, constables,

and other officials in providing a supply of this forced
labor by "law."

"Some of the whites," said an investigator, "had
not outgrown the idea that in some way they were
entitled to the labor of the Negro, and were justified
in getting it at as small an outlay as possible. Planters even agreed to take the entire output of criminals
from some minor rural courts."[1] This number, of
course, could be increased at will, for Negroes were
arrested on such trivial offenses as "swearing before
females, shooting across a public road, carrying ra-
zors, stealing a ride on the train, loitering in a depot,
letting a master's mule bite some other man's corn,
and the like." Then came the question of going to
jail or working out the fine, which some interested
white man stood ready to pay if the convicted person
would only "touch the pen to a contract that was
practically a consent to slavery."[2]

In many cases, too, white as well as black men have
been arrested on flimsy charges, fined and let out to
labor camps to work out their fines. There are cited
cases when the employer present encouraged the defendant to plead guilty with the encouragement that
he would pay his fine and take him into his employ to
work it out. A written acknowledgment of the debt
is secured from the victim in which he agrees to work
for the person paying the fine either on his plantation
or in his labor camp. Taking up his task of working
out the debt, the laborer soon finds himself "charged
with all kinds of goods, and the debt is held over him
for an indefinite period. If, on the other hand, he
revolts and escapes, he is run down by bloodhounds,

---

[1] *Independent*, LV, 1616-1618.
[2] *Ibid.*

arrested without process, returned to the private
prison and probably beaten brutally, because some of
the contracts indirectly provide for all of this."[1]

This situation continued without much question until about a generation ago. Peonage had a fine chance
to flourish without interruption, for the "crimes"
coming before the many justices of the peace involved

SNOW WHITE COTTON

were not reported on to higher authority. In Alabama
the law did not require it. Thousands of individuals
might be arrested, convicted, and sent to the chain
gang without the world knowing it. The justices of
peace, too, might appoint constables who could exercise the same power. A few complaining Negroes
had spoken of these conditions from time to time, but
secured no hearing. Having heard the woes of the
Negroes from time immemorial, the molders of public

[1] *Ibid.*

opinion paid little attention to what they said to individuals or expressed in their indignation meetings. The Negroes of that day had no worthwhile press of their own, and the metropolitan dailies ignored their story. Finally when peonage became so bad as to involve white victims an investigation was ordered by Federal and State governments. Newspapers and magazines carried these accounts as their leading features and an awakened public stood aghast and inquired "can it be so?"[1]

[1] Some of these cases are interesting. S. M. Clyatt, of Tifton, Georgia, was convicted at Tallahassee, Florida, in 1902 in the United States Circuit Court, of coming into Florida with armed men and the assistance of the sheriff of Levy County, Florida, and arresting two Negroes who had run away from his turpentine farm while indebted to him. The men were forcibly apprehended, taken out of the State without legal process and compelled to resume work on the defendant's turpentine farm. A writer says he saw a whole family of white persons including young children forced at the muzzle of a gun to leave their home and return to the swamp labor camp of the father's former employer some miles distant, there to remain until a small indebtedness due the employer was worked out by the father at wages which the employer arbitrarily fixed.

To show how peonage was operating to enslave also the white man the papers published in 1909 the story of the peon Joseph Callas, a Russian Jew. (*Collier's*, July 24, 1909. Vol. 43, p. 26.) He was caught "beating" his way across the country from New York to California in quest of employment. At Little Rock, Arkansas, he was arrested. He was locked up and the next day fined $10. Others arrested for such offenses were shipped with him to a labor camp in Southeast Arkansas. The expenses of the travel were charged to the prisoners. When they reached the camp, although the railway fare was only $6.40, each owed $90. From the railroad station they were conducted by six armed Negroes and a whipping boss and one Gentry, the superintendent, through a forest to a labor camp. At first there were eighty-five men, white and black. They went out to work the next day, two armed Negroes in front, two behind, on one side the overseer with a large whip, in the rear a Negro with a pack of bloodhounds. They were put to gathering cotton, the overseer expressing his anger at the unwilling workers with his whip, sometimes using the butt of it. One white man tried to escape, but he was shot down. They settled down to gathering cotton, felling trees, clearing fields, building fences. The number of whites increased to 45 and Negro victims to 100 in two months. The general order of the camp was two

In 1903 the Federal Grand Jury at Montgomery, Alabama, handed up about a hundred indictments for peonage. One Robert N. Franklin, a kidnaping constable, was indicted on four charges, and J. W. Pace, the manager of a convict camp, who was in collusion with the former in receiving his victims. Pace con-

or three flogged every day, sometimes by a drunken boss, only two meals, one at nine and another at three; the men were always hungry. Forty-five men were lodged in one small room with no comforts or furniture. No medical attention but the doctor's pills which he gave for all ailments. The first overseer was discharged for excessive cruelty. There came in his place an older man who seriously disliked the Negroes and flogged them. If a Negro said anything to him he would beat him on his head with the handle of his whip. Callas wrote letters which finally reached the State Department and an official came for him and exposed the horrors.

Another case is interesting. One Kline of Oklahoma, holding a subcontract for construction work on the Norfolk and Southern Railway in 1907, employed several hundred men, among whom were fifty or sixty foreigners, Russian Poles. He had advanced their railway rates from New York to Greenville, North Carolina, the site of his camp. The foreign laborers became dissatisfied and ceased working without discharging their debt to him. He thereupon applied for redress to the local justice of peace who issued warrants for the arrest of these Russian Poles under the law of North Carolina which permitted imprisonment for obtaining goods or money by false pretenses. They were informed that they had to do one of three things—pay Kline, return to work, or stand criminal trial. They were told that if convicted they would be sentenced to hard labor in the county chain gang to work on the public roads in shackles and without pay. Forty-one elected to go to jail, and the others returned to work. Some of those held paid the money which Kline had advanced and were released. The rest weakened while in custody. Put to shoveling dirt on the road, they felt inclined to notify Kline that they were willing to return to his services and he sent for them. Yet not one of them ever had a trial upon the charge named in the warrant. (*Outlook*, Vol. 87, pp. 319-323.)

Immigrants were, therefore, told by their home countries to stay away from certain states where peonage or similar conditions obtained. (*The Nation*, X, 85, p. 557.) The Italian Government after the experience of seeing their subjects enslaved and slain in Louisiana warned the natives of Italy to stay away from the South. Investigations conducted by its agents showed that "Dagoes" were on par with "Niggers." Austria and Hungary thus blacklisted Missouri and Mississippi. South Carolina and Georgia had boldly declared that they were going to solve the race problem by importing foreigners fessed that he had bought such victims and paid as much as $70 apiece for them. And he forced them to do whatever he told them to do.

One said in referring to the brutal practice of whipping Negroes, "We have to do it once in a while. A Negro ran away from me and hid on the next plantation, eleven miles away. I went after him with my Negro foreman. I took him out of the cabin with a revolver in my hand and drove him home. There I took it out of him with a buggy whip, while the Negro foreman held him. That sounds very shocking to you, no doubt, but I am telling you the facts. If you were the only responsible white man on a plantation and were surrounded by more than five hundred Negroes of the most debased and ignorant character, who cannot be reached by any moral suasion, who are influenced by neither gratitude nor resentment, you would go to the field every day with a revolver in your pocket, as every one of us planters is forced to do, and you would either maintain discipline in the only way the Negro understands it, or else you would give up your plantation to your creditors or your executors, as the case may be." [1]

Another such peonist of Alabama asserted on this wise, "Whether Judge Jones has declared this law constitutional or not, the planters in the black belt will have to maintain their right to reclaim their con-

en masse. A German ship actually brought a cargo of immigrants to Charleston.

The economic extinction of the Negro was proclaimed as at hand. The adversely criticized planters said to the North, "You have misunderstood and misrepresented us when we were attacking a problem in the only way that it can be approached; and in all our so-called maltreatment of the Negroes it is not worse than your white slave traffic, or the Italians working under padrones on the Northern Pacific."

[1] *The Outlook*, Vol. LXXIV, pp. 687-688.

tract labor, or else they will have to go out of business.
Under any other system you would find it impossible

COTTON PICKING AT CLOSER RANGE

to get in your cotton, because the Negroes at the
critical time would simply sit down and refuse to
work. When they are well we compel our laborers to

go to the field by force. This is the truth and there is
no use lying about it.''

Nowhere in the country, however, has peonage been
accepted by a majority of the people except probably in the Mississippi and Red River lowlands, in
middle and South Georgia, in Alabama, and in the
backward parts of South Carolina, like Bamberg
County. Laws which permitted it were enacted by

THE OLD LOG CABIN

a coterie representing the interests rather than the
people. It obtained only where the rich planters
thus interested could control both the political and
economic forces of the community. There were counties in which most of the planters practiced peonage
in some fashion, but there were not whole States
where the majority of the people were thus depraved.
In the course of time, too, when thinking people became thoroughly aware of the consequences of the

evil they set their faces against it, and during the last generation have done much to exterminate the institution.

Peonage as it now exists, moreover, has been extensively mollified. The public may wink at the system as long as it does not show excessive cruelty. For example, according to the report of Governor Dorsey's investigation of such crimes, there were other peonists in Georgia when Williams of Jasper County was caught in the act of unmercifully whipping and cruelly murdering peons who did not do his biddings and of forcing certain peons to kill those who were rebellious. The papers of the country were filled with the accounts of his inhuman practices. Feeling against him ran rather high, and he was convicted and sent to the penitentiary.[1] The objection here was not so much one against peonage as against the shotgun, bloodhound sort of peonage which Williams practiced.[2]

[1] *A Statement from Governor Hugh M. Dorsey as to the Negro in Georgia.*

[2] Not only were other peons in Georgia at that time, but they have been found there since. An educated native visiting a certain part of Georgia, in 1920, said:

"The question of labor in the part of the country where I live is quite different from that which obtains here. We have no labor unions; we have no large, established industries in which to find our people work, but we are mostly farmers and we deal directly with the red-nosed Georgia cracker on the farm, and the bulk of the labor there is ignorant. The Negroes there have been the victims of crooks who prey upon their ignorance. They get them to sign labor contracts and hold out to them large possibilities at the beginning of the year, move them to their farms, and furnish them with such things as they need to begin with. In a few months, when the crops are almost made, they shut down. In too many instances I have met my people with as many as six to twelve in family. They had worked a year, the head of the family had been charged with some petty crime, and they had been driven from their farms.

"The white farmer has taken advantage of conditions that have grown out of the war, and as he gives the laborer better wages, he

Peonage, however, is far from being a thing of the past. Although these laws authorizing peonage have been declared unconstitutional the Federal Government is powerless in the South in the protection of the Negroes in the enjoyment of citizenship. The planters, moreover, are a law unto themselves. The planters enforcing peonage have gone down to such a low point in the social ladder that they do not think seriously of public opinion as a restraining force. If a man of influence in the cotton or sugar section wants to violate a law, he can usually find some way to do it. The main instrument depended upon to effect the desired reform has been education, an effort to teach men humanity and to convince them of the futility of forced labor. Such a method of attack requires time, for the persons thus engaged in the uneconomic practice will be the last to see the errors of their ways and to act in the interests of the public good rather than for selfish purposes.[1]

Unfortunately, certain planters have developed so far in that direction that they cannot think of solving

runs up the rent in proportion to the increase of wages, so that the black man on the farm is practically just where he was before the war. If I rented a farm for 1,500 pounds of cotton last year and that cotton went up to thirty-five cents, the owner went back and put on a thousand pounds more. The owner will demand not diversified farming, but will so arrange it that you cannot farm intensively. You must plant cotton. You cannot plant and work a grain crop.

"Another feature is that when these people sign these contracts, they find themselves all tied up, and the man in the family tries to get himself out by running away somewhere. A warrant is sworn out and that man is hunted down, arrested and locked in chains and brought back and put in jail. He is incarcerated for the next two years. Not one, not two, but scores of instances have been brought to me. This condition obtains in Early County, Dooly County, Worth County, Decatur County, Toombs County, and Morgan County."—*The Crisis*, XX, 139 (July, 1920).

[1] *Herald-Commonwealth*, November 30, 1929 (quoting *The New York World*).

their problem any other way; and the Negroes so
long accustomed to the forced labor have too often
come to regard this as their permanent status. Some
of them have gone so far down in efficiency that they
would not succeed in making a living independently.
They have lost their initiative or they have never
had the opportunity to develop any. A few years ago
a peon of this class was taken by a Southern family

AN ISLAND HOME IN SOUTH CAROLINA

to serve them for life in New Jersey. Public spirited
citizens, having found out that there was a case of
involuntary servitude in their midst, protested and
interceded in behalf of the peon. The Negro girl
was taken away from the white family and placed in
another home where she would have the freedom formerly denied her. A few days thereafter the girl
expressed herself as being tired of her independent
life. She had been dependent on others so long that
she doubted her ability to provide properly for all of
her needs. She grieved to get back to her master

and pined away as a result of this forced estrange-
ment. It became necessary, therefore, for her friends
to abandon all plans for her future that she might
return to the stream for which her heart had long
panted. The effort in her behalf was futile. It was
a case of love's labor lost. And so it is to-day with
many other peons in the United States.[1]

THE FRUIT OF INDUSTRY

On the contrary, however, in October, 1919, Negroes
of Elaine, Arkansas, rebelled against peonage. They
were attacked, and because they fought back a number
of them were shot down. By local and State authority
the others were finally overpowered, arrested and
tried for high crimes. Sixty-seven were sentenced
to long terms of imprisonment and twelve to death
by a mob court going through the mockery of trial.

[1] This account appeared in various weekly newspapers in 1928.

Their cases were appealed and six of the twelve got a stay of execution on the ground that the court did not state the degree of murder of which they were guilty. The case attracted national attention as an effort to annihilate innocent people who had done no more than strike for economic freedom. An exposé of the matter showed that it was such a flagrant act of injustice that upon appeal to Federal courts the State tribunals were reversed and those peons convicted of murder were released.

Negroes, too, sometimes interfere in behalf of friends and relatives. In 1923 Emma Johnson and her two little girls, berry-pickers of Picayune, Mississippi, were enticed by a labor agent and a colored woman to Tangipahoa Parish, Louisiana, with the promise of transportation and board and pay of one cent for every box of strawberries picked. They were finally conducted to the strawberry farm of Benjamin Kincheon, nine miles from Tickfaw, where they were held in bondage. Hezzie Pringle, Emma Johnson's brother, having found out where she was and the State in which she was serving, made way to the farm and tried to secure their release. He offered to pay whatever debt they owed, but he was beaten over the head by Kincheon who would have shot him, if his wife had not interfered by holding the revolver until Pringle could escape. Arriving at New Orleans, he informed the Federal authorities who had the peons released.[1]

The disturbance of the conditions by the Mississippi flood revealed a state of peonage which was all but general there. Negro refugees had to be taken from the plantations to the Red Cross Camp set up as

1 *The Crisis*, XXVI, 128.

asylums for the sufferers. The planters seriously objected to having these peons removed by the Red Cross, because at first they did not think the flood would last long; and the planters yielded only on the condition that the Red Cross would return these Negroes to them and would not let labor agents entice them away. Negroes, therefore, were let out of these camps only upon requests of planters presenting to

A Barn of a Successful Farmer to Hold the Fruits of Labor for Better Prices

the Red Cross workers lists of their "niggers." The peons could not leave the camps without passes. The only hope for escape was to run away before their "owners" called for them. This they found difficult in face of the national guard stationed at the camps to hold the peons for the plantations and to force them to work by cursing, kicking, beating, and occasionally killing them. When these camps were broken up the Red Cross did not nominally force the

Negroes to return to the plantation but worked it thus
by refusing to give them transportation to any other
place unless they had received letters showing that
they would be taken care of by friends and relatives
elsewhere. As few could do this, the only alterna-
tive was to return to the plantations to continue in
peonage.[1]

Peonage, too, may be discovered where you would
least expect it. For example, in 1928, Thelma Duncan, a teacher, found peons in one of the rural districts of North Carolina, in a State where more is
being done for the uplift of the Negro than in any
other Southern parts. She found families of Negroes
bound to white landlords for debts which they were
never permitted to pay. They remain there in this
state, uneducated, unenlightened, not knowing what is
going on in the world, and believing that they must
remain forever in the slave relation which they sustain to their planters.[2] There comes little light upon
their pathway, and they would hardly know how to
heed the call if they were told that the world is theirs
if they would go forth and possess it.

[1] Letter of Captain J. A. G. of the Mississippi National Guard in
The Crisis, January. 1928.
[2] Statement made to the author by Thelma Duncan.

CHAPTER V

INDUSTRY AND TRADE

IN spite of the undesirable conditions exhibited by the prevalence of crop tenancy and peonage some rural Negroes have also the chance to earn a livelihood in industry. Along with these people on the farm, of course, are Negro mechanics and artisans. Of these there are many more than one would expect unless he is well enough acquainted with things to understand the Southern white man's attitude toward work. He believes that labor is not dignified and thus leaves open to the Negroes in that section positions from which they are barred by trades unions in the North and West. The number of such positions, to be sure, is determined by the general needs of the agricultural area and the exceptional demand for skilled labor, which, in case of large contracts, may be brought in from industrial centers. On the plantations themselves, however, there are houses to be constructed, walls to be built, and machinery to be kept in repair. Negro skilled laborers do most of this work. They receive much higher compensation than laborers on the farms, usually from $1.50 to $2.50 a day; but, being at the mercy of their employers, they dare not ask for and never dream of receiving such compensation as is given labor of this kind in the large industrial centers. Persons have advocated the organization of these

89

workers in unions, but those in the remote districts
are not sufficiently enlightened to understand such
appeals, and their contact with the outer world is so
slight that these thoughts do not reach them. These
mechanics and artisans, like the agricultural workers,
moreover, are thoroughly dominated by the terror-
striking planter class.

In small towns of even not more than 2,000 or 3,000

CHILDREN OF THE TOMOKA MISSION IN THE TURPENTINE DISTRICT IN
FLORIDA

population, however, there is considerable industry
to attract Negro skilled labor not always controlled
by the planters. The promoters of the plants in such
towns may not be dependent upon the surrounding
farmers and thus may not be dominated at all by
them. In some cases, however, they have such con-
nections, and must take into account the attitude of
these neighbors. The Negro skilled laborers thus
engaged in these towns have a higher economic status
than those restricted to the distant plantations. Such

workers are in closer touch with the world. They have larger opportunities for travel and the exchange of ideas. They are, therefore, more independent than the Negro mechanics and artisans of the backwoods and receive more consideration from their employers.

That some of these town industries are seasonal is often the salvation of both the farmer and the promoter of industry. Sometimes when the two are controlled by the same owners things work out exactly as they would have them. The production of the crop comes at one time and the industry opens somewhat later in the year. In some cases this develops naturally. The canning of fruits and vegetables cannot take place before they are produced, cotton compression must follow cotton production, and fishing is better if deferred for a certain time of the year. Negroes in these sections, then, work on the farm during the summer and go into the industries for the fall and winter. This gives them year-round employment, but they receive lower wages than they would if this industry were operated in competition with agriculture.

In recent years the opportunity for the Negroes in industry has become more general in the Upper South as a result of the transplantation of manufacturing from the East to the places of the raw materials in the South. The effort to ruralize the city and to urbanize the country has also had an important bearing. For adequate space, lower rents and the opportunity for independent growth, too, certain industries are leaving the cities for the country. In this the rural Negro has figured from the very beginning of this industrialization. In the main, Negroes have served as common laborers, but in many of these enterprises they have engaged in both semi-skilled and skilled labor. In a few liberal sections of the South, then, where tenancy and peonage are not enforced as the unwritten law of the planters, Negro laborers have a choice between working on the farm and serving in some industry. The wages paid these Negroes fall below what such laborers receive in the East; but, being higher than the wages paid on the

A COTTON GIN

farms, some planters have had to increase wages to meet the competition of growing industry.

The extent to which the South has been recently industrialized cannot be easily judged from the latest figures. The United States Bureau of the Census reports do not show much change from 1923 to 1925. In some states there was a decrease; in others an increase. The figures of recent years, however, show

TABLE II—INDUSTRIAL ESTABLISHMENTS IN THE SOUTH IN 1925 TOGETHER WITH THE NUMBER OF WAGE EARNERS AND THE AMOUNT PAID.[1]

1925	Number	Wage Earners	Wages
Alabama	2,349	116,599	$101,242,839
Arkansas	1,257	43,977	37,538,492
Florida	1,863	66,204	65,780,109
Delaware	419	20,704	25,072,302
Georgia	2,876	141,173	99,210,003
Kentucky	1,864	76,580	84,945,679
Louisiana	1,742	88,058	79,762,794
Maryland	3,184	125,787	138,590,634
Mississippi	1,705	55,171	41,231,045
Missouri	5,114	194,959	230,690,902
North Carolina	2,614	182,234	134,237,097
Oklahoma	1,282	26,333	34,210,630
South Carolina	1,134	100,144	67,061,783
Tennessee	2,162	107,645	95,255,480
Texas	3,606	106,792	116,363,302
Virginia	2,553	112,135	105,886,599
West Virginia	1,395	80,700	105,892,102

a tremendous gain over the status of industry reported in 1914. In most cases the number of establishments have decreased, as would be naturally expected in the passing or in the combination of war time enterprises; but while the number of wage earners have also decreased, the amount of their earnings have increased. This, of course, is due not altogether to the closing down of plants, but also to the rapid mechanization now going on in the industrial world. In 1914 there were in the Southern States, where more than three-fourths of the Negroes toil, 64,138 establishments and 2,313,852 wage earners, receiving wages to the amount of $616,375,766. In 1925 these had changed so as to have 37,657 establishments and 1,654,548 wage earners receiving $1,578,391,859. In this case both the wage earners

[1] United States Census of Manufactures, 1925.

and the number of establishments decreased, but the wages paid increased more than 125 per cent.[1]

Not all of these persons, to be sure, are Negroes; but the large majority of those engaged as common laborers belong to this race. In a few cases, however, Negroes are employed to operate machinery as in two of the knitting mills in Suffolk, Virginia.[2] The

SHOEING THE ANIMAL

rising industrial centers of the South, then, have attracted Negroes from the farms; and from these smaller establishments the Negroes have migrated to larger centers of the North and East to satisfy their desire for still higher wages. A considerable number of these rural Negroes, however, never leave the farms permanently but spend their time alternately

[1] United States Census of Manufactures, 1925.
[2] This fact was determined by actual observation of three investigators.

between the town and country, availing themselves of the most profitable season of high wages in each case.

In industry, in general, it is sometimes a little difficult to determine exactly how conspicuously Negroes in the South figure in this sphere. In certain enterprises mainly restricted to the country because of their very nature, the problem is much easier in such cases as the making of clay products, lumbering, turpentine and resin production, mining, wood distillation, quarrying, canning, and fishing. With the exception of such industries in the upper South or the Border States of Delaware, Maryland, West Virginia, and possibly Kentucky, Virginia, and Tennessee, these enterprises are conducted mainly with Negro labor; and even in some of these states the Negroes share equally the honor with the whites.[1]

The statistics for mining and quarrying in 1919 showed 4,440 establishments and 296,112 wage earners receiving $353,266,560. The manufacturing census of 1925, however, gives later figures for these other interests. In the production of things from clay at that time there were engaged 532 establishments employing 26,533 workers who were receiving $4,472,-142. In canning fish, crabs, shrimps, etc., there were 87 establishments employing 3,261 workers, paid $1,104,326. In preserving fruits and vegetables there were 751 establishments and 13,562 workers, paid $7,795,124. In lumbering were 5,560 establishments with 257,115 workers, paid $222,704,493. In wood distillation were 19 establishments with 1,421

[1] These data and subsequent figures in this chapter were compiled from various bulletins issued by the United States Bureau of the Census with respect to these industries herein mentioned.

TABLE III—DISTRIBUTION OF CERTAIN INDUSTRIES IN THE SOUTH
THE NUMBER OF EM

	Clay Products (other than pottery) and non-clay refractories			Canning and preserving fish, crabs, shrimp, oysters and clams			Canning and preserving: fruits and vegetables; pickles, jellies, preserves, and sauces		
	Num-ber	Wage Earners	Wages	Num-ber	Wage Earners	Wages	Num-ber	Wage Earners	Wages
Alabama...........	38	2,094	$1,662,828	5	167	$77,731	5	132	$60,420
Arkansas...........	13	526	474,168	.....	....	....	51	822	292,853
Delaware...........	7	96	91,529	.....	....	....	55	1,261	892,455
Florida...........	9	154	106,145	12	284	122,118	8	107	76,492
Georgia...........	31	2,652	1,834,259	11	485	88,489	7	121	55,941
Kentucky...........	42	2,642	2,751,912	.....	....	....	26	994	670,193
Louisiana...........	17	382	318,681	20	835	283,340	14	272	100,995
Maryland...........	26	1,293	1,313,969	.....	....	....	322	6,949	3,975,552
Mississippi.........	23	501	373,148	18	784	361,031	8	325	110,109
Missouri...........	62	5,734	6,753,389	.....	....	....	105	1,767	849,864
North Carolina......	64	1,724	1,212,146	4	68	16,159	.....	....	....
Oklahoma...........	17	685	671,979	.....	....	....	3	30	12,909
South Carolina......	23	938	591,656	6	509	103,372	.....	....	....
Tennessee...........	35	1,756	1,468,500	.....	....	....	40	616	242,808
Texas..............	54	2,460	1,848,787	.....	....	....	26	249	168,367
Virginia...........	45	1,482	1,316,943	11	129	52,086	81	812	282,166
West Virginia........	26	1,414	1,682,103	.....	....	....	.....	....	....
	532	26,533	$4,472,142	87	3,261	$1,104,326	751	13,562	$7,795,124

District Columbia—No. 3; Wage Earners 12; Wages $8,150.

In the study of this table some explanations may be helpful.
In making the distinction between salaried officers and employees
the statisticians based their classification not upon the unit of
time employed but upon the character of work done. Persons
performing manual labor in addition to supervisory duties are
herein reported as wage earners. The number of such persons
employed on the fifteenth day of each month, or the nearest
representative day, was reported, and the average for the year
was calculated by dividing by 12 the sum of the numbers reported for the several months.
Under wages will be found the total compensation of salaried

EMPLOYING SOME NEGROES, SHOWING THE NUMBER OF ESTABLISHMENTS, PLOYEES AND THEIR WAGES, 1925

Lumber and timber products, not elsewhere classified			Wood distillations and charcoal Manufacture			Turpentine and Rosin			Mines and Quarries (1919)		
Number	Wage Earners	Wages	Number	Wage Earners	Wages	Number	Wage Earners	Wages	Number	Wage Earners	Wages
942	29,095	$18,234,136	4	103	$61,541	97	2,116	$1,145,788	348	32,579	$36,229,723
424	25,217	19,977,983	....	....	....	....	.....	....	126	3,630	4,573,291
16	207	135,955	....	....	....	....	.....	....	8	116	135,502
179	17,777	14,934,251	5	298	215,725	310	10,890	5,864,038	55	3,372	3,107,813
477	14,875	9,147,703	....	....	....	519	12,961	6,371,616	82	2,397	2,017,460
119	3,483	2,889,962	....	....	....	....	.....	....	864	43,563	49,550,588
301	39,241	32,798,404	3	201	225,509	13	1,104	511,493	4	5,228	7,504,657
132	1,429	1,082,178	....	....	....	....	.....	....	161	5,628	6,151,744
917	36,397	26,485,877	4	261	157,654	32	1,661	991,611	....	.....	....
86	4,203	3,588,885	....	....	....	....	.....	....	494	14,857	16,777,353
515	17,787	12,900,303	....	....	....	....	.....	....	106	1,890	1,489,062
28	1,692	1,450,092	....	....	....	....	.....	....	284	33,914	46,809,200
273	15,686	10,305,351	....	....	....	....	.....	....	20	933	680,484
324	11,185	8,550,512	3	558	522,915	....	.....	....	263	14,470	12,987,338
196	18,200	14,949,971	....	....	....	....	.....	....	81	18,164	29,557,997
493	11,621	8,447,487	....	....	....	....	.....	....	216	14,547	16,108,249
138	9,020	9,825,443	....	....	....	....	.....	....	1,325	100,812	119,577,949
5,560	257,115	$272,704,493	19	1,421	1,183,344	971	28,732	14,884,546	4,440	296,112	$353,266,560

officers and employees and the total compensation of wage earners (including those employed on a piece-price basis). The supervisory officers, however, were only a few persons attached to these establishments, although their compensation was disproportionately large.

A fairly reliable standard of the measurement of the growth of industry is afforded by the average number of wage earners, but "it must be remembered that, on the one hand, in some industries mechanical processes have displaced hand labor to such an extent as to make possible a marked increase in production with no increase in the number of wage earners, while, on the other hand, the average length of the working day has been decreasing for many years."

workers, paid $1,183,344.   In the production of
turpentine and resin were 971 establishments and
28,732 workers, paid $14,884,546.

The largest number of Negroes employed in industry in the South are engaged in lumbering.   This
includes the work of logging camps and saw mills.
The statistics given above do not include veneer mills

A DEMONSTRATION IN FORESTRY

and cooperage stock mills.   The workers herein referred to produce in the logging camps such as saw
logs, shingles, staves, heading bolts, hewn and round
poles, mine timbers, spars, piling, fence posts, railway ties, wheel handles, and excelsior stock.   At the
saw mills they produce rough lumber shingles, lath,
sawed railway ties, cooperage, spool, pencil, pen-
holder, and veneer stock.

In addition to being employed in cutting and preparing these lumber products Negroes are also en-

gaged in the transportation of them to market. There is the necessity for bringing these products from the saw mills to navigable streams and railroads. The Negroes are usually active in the transportation of this lumber by water. Wages here are much higher than on the farms although employment is not so nearly permanent as in agriculture. In the case of piece-work the compensation is still greater, but it is almost a pittance compared with pay received in the lumber camps of the Great West. In view of the rapid depletion of the forests in this country during the last two generations one may judge for himself the extent to which this industry has figured in the life of the South and consequently its bearing on the present status of the rural Negroes.

Along with lumbering should be considered the closely related industry of the production of turpentine and resin. This industry comprises the distillation of the semifluid exudation from certain species of pine trees. This product in its first form is called by such various names as crude gum, crude turpentine, and resin. The unit of measure in turpentine wood operations is the "crop." This consists of about 10,500 boxes or cups cut into the trees to drain them of their blood, the gum. The cutting is followed by chipping or removing the bark above the boxes to the extent of twenty-four inches. In certain parts the box system has given place to the metal cup into which the gum is conveyed by means of metal gutters inserted in the tree and leading diagonally downward. Then there is the task of gathering the gum which hardens on the face of the tree. This is called "scrape."

The industry, however, is seasonal. It commences

in the spring when the sap begins to flow. The
months of maximum employment were September in
1924-1925 and May in 1925-1926. The States most
active in such production in 1925 were Alabama,
Florida, Georgia, Louisiana, and Mississippi, with a
little interest in North Carolina, South Carolina, and
Texas. In proportion as the pine forests disap-
pear, of course, the industry must grow less and less.

SPRAYING TO KILL THE INSECTS

In 1925 there were 971 establishments thus engaged
with 28,732 wage earners who received $14,884,546.
The large majority of the workers thus employed in
the South are Negroes, and unfortunately their life
is so uncertain, so movable, going from one seat to
another, that they are kept far down in a most undesirable state, among the lowest of the lowly.

Along with lumbering goes, too, the industry of
wood distillation. Hardwood distillation is confined

mainly to the Northern and Central States; but soft
wood distillation is carried on largely in the South
Atlantic and Gulf States. The Southern longleaf
pine is the principal raw material used in this industry. The plants utilize the slabs, sawdust, and other
waste products of saw mill or timber camps. The
Southern states chiefly concerned with this industry
are Alabama, Florida, Louisiana, Mississippi, and

A LOG CAMP

Tennessee. In 1925 there were 19 establishments
thus engaged and 1,421 workers paid $1,183,344.

Next to lumbering and its correlated interests
comes canning. This falls into two divisions: preserving fruits, vegetables, pickles, jellies, preserves,
and sauces; and the canning of fish, crabs, shrimps,
oysters, and clams. The preservation of fruits and
vegetables is not uncommon in the South. All of
the States where Negroes are found in considerable
numbers except North Carolina, South Carolina, and
West Virginia, report such industries. In some

cases, as in Alabama, Florida, Georgia, Mississippi and Oklahoma, the industry is not considerable. The number of establishments reported in 1925 were 651 with 13,562 workers, paid $7,795,124. It would seem here, as in the case of the canning of fish and the like, that certain centers, where the people are most active in the selling of these things in their fresh state, have not taken readily to the industry of canning.

The industry herein considered does not include the canning of meats, the data for which are given under meat-packing, not much of which is carried on in the South. It should be noted here, too that the canning of fish and the like would naturally be restricted to those States bordering on productive waters, namely, such Southern States as Alabama, Florida, Georgia, Louisiana, Mississippi, North Carolina, South Carolina, and Virginia. In Maryland where such an industry might be expected to take root it seems that the people are primarily engaged in the more lucrative line of this industry, selling of fish in the fresh state. No such activity is reported for Arkansas, Delaware, Kentucky, Missouri, Oklahoma, Tennessee, Texas, and West Virginia. The number of establishments thus engaged in 1925 were 87 with 3,261 workers paid $1,104,326.

The fisheries of the country engage a considerable number of Negroes. The extent to which they are employed cannot be accurately determined. A helpful estimate may be made, however, by keeping in mind the area of this industry and the value of its productions. The latest statistics for the Mississippi River and its tributaries published by the United States Fish Commission in 1922 give 19,122 persons, equipment worth $7,356,034, and products valued at $4,503,521. Statistics for Maryland and Virginia give 25,856 persons engaged, equipment worth $10,635,397, and products valued at $13,948,060. In Delaware in 1926 there were 1,508 persons thus engaged and the products worth $269,780. On the Gulf Coast including Florida, Alabama, Mississippi, Louisiana, and Texas, there were 15,133 persons en-

HOME ECONOMICS DEMONSTRATION IN THE COUNTRY

gaged in 1927 and products valued at $4,127,137, together with a catch of shellfish and miscellaneous products worth $5,838,638. In this work Negroes do most of the drudgery.

Clay products (other than pottery) and non-clay refractories pottery next claim the attention of the observer of the Negroes in industry. In every Southern State where Negroes constitute a considerable portion of the population this industry is found. This includes brick, tile, earthenware, and the like. In the passing of the forest and at the same time the rise of the city as an attraction of the rural population, this industry becomes more important and a larger number of Negroes have been drawn into it. It is about as costly now to build of wood as it is of brick. Inasmuch as homes must be built of something this industry assumes larger proportions, and those in it are assured of permanent employment. In this industry, too, as in the case of others once located elsewhere, many establishments are developing preferably in the South where proximity to the raw materials reduces the cost by keeping down the expense of transportation.

A still larger number of Negroes are engaged in mines and quarries. We have no available statistics of these industries since 1919 when they were rather high as a result of the multiplication of enterprises during the World War, after which so many perished in the slump in business in 1921. In 1919 there were in the South 4,440 establishments with 296,112 workers, paid $353,266,560. The Negroes thus engaged were largely the iron ore workers in Virginia, Tennessee, and Alabama, and the coal miners of Alabama, Arkansas, Virginia, Kentucky, and West Virginia. In the granite quarries of Georgia, North Carolina, and South Carolina Negroes are found in a conspicuous position; also in the phosphate rock mining of Florida and Tennessee. They are likewise employed in the production of lead and zinc in Missouri, Oklahoma, and Tennessee; in mining sulphur in Texas; and in the extraction of petroleum and natural gas in Texas, Oklahoma, Kentucky, and West Virginia. Outside of this rural area in what is known as Southern Pennsylvania, Southern Ohio, and Southern Indiana some use is also made of Negroes in these industries. While the whites operate most of the machinery and do most of the skilled labor Negroes do most of the dangerous and laborious work.

Numerous minor industries closely connected with agriculture, the chief concern of the South, require

THE CATTLE AT HOME

some menial labor which Negroes in the main supply. These are such as the ginning of cotton, cotton compressing, making up the cotton into bales, and the production of oil and fertilizers from the seed of the cotton. The rural Negroes engaged in agriculture during other seasons of the year readily shift to this industry when they are not hindered by troublesome contracts requiring all of their time on the plantations or when the planters, still a law unto themselves, do not force them to abstain from such engagements. In the very backward districts only would such a shift of labor be prevented by these illegal methods.

Some few other rural Negroes find an outlet through such employment as driving teams across the country, long distance hauling, loading and un-

PROUD OF THE STOCK

loading trains and boats, dredging streams, building bridges, and keeping the roads in repair. Here again we find the same rule followed. The whites have the contracts to do these things, and they hire Negroes to perform most of the work.

In the town stores and at the plantation commissary, too, the white man is in charge, but the Negro must be there to do the work. After the clerk drives the bargain in exchanging so much raw material for goods the Negro employee must check up on the material supplied and measure out the articles for which it is exchanged. The white man is supposed to supply the brains and the Negro the muscle. Often the white does not furnish either, but the Negro cannot hold his job unless he is equal to what is required of him.

This diversification of labor is wholesome in breaking up the monotony of agriculture and offering fur-

POULTRY RAISING OF A LATER DAY

ther competition in the interest of higher wages. Negroes thus employed, moreover, have other opportunities for improvement and advancement resulting from frequent contact with the busy world and some little participation in carrying out its commercial program. They greet passengers on the way, observe how they dress, how they conduct themselves, and what they do in the struggle of life. The trade of the section passes in review before them and opens their eyes as to what is going on in the industrial sphere. From this comes an urge to migrate to points where more is to be seen and enjoyed, and workers from the plantations must be drawn to these positions thus made vacant by seekers of fortune in other quarters.

In the case of seasonal industry, too, the Negroes in the rural districts participate not only as laborers but as contractors. Negro farmers whose teams are no longer needed on the farm take contracts to haul lumber, sand, gravel, and the like for which there is often a larger demand than the regular facilities of local transportation can supply when some unexpected rural industry develops. The income from such work is sometimes considerable, sufficient to make up for the deficiency of short crops, to purchase additional land, or to bring a larger area under cultivation. Such farmers depend more generally, however, upon hauling to market what their own lands yield of sumac, sassafras root, tan bark, or railroad ties. Upon the sale of such products many of these farmers of the Upper South are so dependent that they do not wait for certain seasons of the year to market such things, but they stop their work at certain intervals during the month to carry these things to town to exchange them for groceries and other supplies needed throughout the planting and harvesting season. Saturday is the day of the week when most of them drive these bargains. All along the road to and from the town used to appear the heavily loaded ox carts and wagons, changed now to a procession of trucks which hurry things onward in more modern fashion. The procession is social as well as material. There are exchanges of ideas, reports on the state of the crops, discussions of the prospective prices, and the gossip about the good or evil fortunes of those who have plunged beyond the customary mark.

CHAPTER VI

IN spite of these untoward conditions rural Negroes have not always given up the struggle as hopeless. Some by dint of energy have risen above the average condition. Others have been favored by circumstances. Here and there in these parts, then, one finds the Negro occasionally undertaking everything the white man does, developing into planters, becoming merchants, and engaging in manufacturing. In some of these instances the task is well done; in others success has not followed. To explain the failures need not detain us here to repeat a rather well-known story. It is sufficient to remark that the white men, being first on the ground before Negroes in large numbers were free to engage in these things, preëmpted the field and with larger capital and multifarious advantages over the Negroes they have easily held the lead until now. Occasionally, however, the Negro planter, trader, or manufacturer in competition with whites have surpassed them in the business and thoroughly established themselves.[1]

Of such there may be cited a number of interesting examples. Shivers of Smithfield, Virginia, noted for its hams, has the largest and best equipped provision

[1] The data herein presented were compiled largely from actual observation of various investigators employed for such research. Other data came from directories, accounts of enterprising men, and commercial reports. Hundreds of persons were interviewed with respect to reported achievements in order to check up on such reports. In some cases one investigator followed the other to test his work.

store in that town. He ships meats to points as far away as Boston. W. P. Evans, of Laurinburg, North Carolina, has made just as favorable an impression with his general store in that town, and with his earnings he has been able to figure prominently in other commercial ventures. Scott Bond, of Arkansas, has established his reputation as a planter and at the same time developed a prosperous commission merchant

WORKING ON THE ROAD

business in a nearby town. The Huberts in Georgia have succeeded in getting hold of and developing hundreds of acres of land in Georgia, which have yielded income to maintain a family of sixteen children who have gone to college and have rendered efficient service in different walks of life in various parts of the country. The late J. G. Groves, of Edwardsville, Kansas, so far surpassed his neighbors in the production of potatoes that he became known as the

"Potato King," and his son has endeavored to keep his interests intact.

The Negroes' best opportunities for struggling upward in these lines, however, have been in settlements and towns largely restricted to the black population. These centers appear from State to State where there is a natural preponderance of Negroes or where because of favorable circumstances they have concen-

THE NEW HOME IN THE MAKING

trated at certain points. Yet in the Lower South, especially in South Carolina and Mississippi, where the rural Negroes outnumber the whites, they are kept in such a backward condition that their large numbers have not meant very much for the higher strivings in the economic world. The Negroes in smaller numbers in rural communities elsewhere have done just as well or better in these spheres. Here, of course, it is evident that unless the people are sufficiently enlightened to have some vision there can be no hope for constructive efforts upward. Mound Bayou in Mississippi is an exception to this rule in that section.

These Negro towns and settlements, however, are generally referred to not as evidence of what the Negro can do but of what he cannot do. Lack of wealth and enterprise has prevented them from developing. Their growth is so slow that they do not

NEIGHBORS

attract the element of Negroes needed for their economic welfare. White men shun them because of the prejudice against dwelling among Negroes unless there happens to be an unusual opportunity for business which they feel they cannot afford to neglect. Such white business men commanding more capital and credit than Negroes sometimes thus thrive on Negro settlements. They may not live exactly within the Negro group, but near enough by to attract the trade. With the advantages already pointed out they can undercut the Negro entrepreneur and force him out of business. Yet these white merchants, although drawing off the wealth of the Negro settlement, contribute nothing to the upbuilding of the community. What surplus they have to invest outside of their business goes into something in a community controlled by their own race.

Negro settlements and towns are not restricted to

A Sign of Prosperity

the South where most Negroes are found. In proportion to the population just as many or more are found in the North and West. In these two sections it has sometimes been necessary for Negroes to settle together for mutual protection, when such a group in the South might be dispersed over a larger area. In some rural communities outside of the South Negroes are not permitted to live at all. In several cases after becoming settled here and there, Negroes have been driven out of communities in the North

and West as it recently happened to about 400
Negroes expelled from North Platte, Nebraska, because one of their race happened to kill a policeman.

Some of the Northern Negro settlements are far
from being new. The Bassett, Cabin Creek, Greenville, Roberts, Weaver, and Lost Creek settlements in
Indiana resulted from the efforts of Quakers in North
Carolina, who about a century ago freed their slaves

THE HOME OF THE NEW TYPE OF FARMER

and transplanted them to Southern Indiana. The
Long, McIntyre, and Randolph settlements in Ohio
and that of Calvin Township in Michigan, owe their
origin mainly to the efforts of sympathetic whites
similarly interested. Many other such settlements in
the free States were broken up between 1850 and
1861 by a rigid execution of the fugitive slave law.
Other such settlements of less significance are Deer-
field in Colorado, Brownlee in Nebraska, and Snow

Hill in New Jersey, all of a different development.

In the South, one would hardly think of Negro settlements since Negroes are found almost everywhere the whites live, but there are some places in the South where one does not find more whites than Negroes. In Virginia there is Averett, in Mecklenburg County, developed largely with George D. Wharton as the

RURAL TEACHERS ATTENDING THE SUMMER SCHOOL OF THE WEST VIRGINIA STATE COLLEGE, INSTITUTE, WEST VIRGINIA

moving spirit, serving as planter, merchant, postmaster, and minister. Still more interesting is Method, North Carolina, not far from Raleigh, a settlement owing its rise largely to the acumen of the unusual planter and business man, Berry O. Kelly, well known and highly respected throughout that State. In Alabama are Baldwin Farms and the Southern Improvement Settlement in Limestone

County, the prosperity of which is due largely to the development of agriculture stimulated from Tuskegee. Then there is one distinctly Negro community in Arkansas called Peace, and for various reasons the majority of the whites around have agreed to let them have it. Mississippi has three interesting settlements known as Des Velente, Chambers, and New Africa, not too far removed from the old.

There are in the South, of course, various other settlements where the Negroes constitute the majority of the population. In all of these, however, they have not been permitted to go their own way. Such groupings are Negro settlements in spite of themselves. They are places where Negroes are permitted to dwell and sometimes where they must dwell or leave the section. The whites control everything, but the Negroes find it better there than elsewhere among strangers whom they can reach only with the great difficulty of breaking up their homes and trying their fortunes far away.

In the case of actual Negro towns the dominance of the race is more apparent. There is more group effort, and one has a better chance to study what has thus been accomplished by coöperation. In the North and West there are not as many Negro towns as settlements. Whenever the settlement has shown the possibility of urban organization the whites with more facilities for such efforts have usually stepped in to control it, or they have managed to keep Negroes away from those strategic points where such was possible. One hears of Abila, Allensworth, and Bowles, in Fresno County, and Victorville in San Bernardino County, California; of Brooklyn and Robbins in Illinois; of Nicodemus in Graham County,

Kansas; of Marlborough in Michigan; and of Gould-
town and Springtown in Cumberland County, New
Jersey, and Whitesboro, near Cape May, in the same
State. Some of these like Idlewild, Michigan, and
Highland Beach in Maryland, however, are merely
summer resorts open only during that season ‘in
imitation of places which do not welcome Negroes.

A COUNTRY BEAUTY AFTER THE
MILKING

THE DESK OF A FARMER

These towns do as well as can be expected, for they
exist solely on what the Negroes are able to spend
for luxury after providing for the necessities of life.
In the impecunious condition of most Negroes, the
amount of money which they can spare for such purposes is limited and towns thus maintained necessarily have a precarious future.

Negro towns of the South are not much larger than

those of the North although most Negroes are in that section. The agricultural development of the South has not been so conducive to urbanization as industry has been elsewhere. Interesting, however, are the Alabama towns of Cedarlake in Morgan County, Greenwood Village in Macon County, Plateau near Mobile, and Shepherdsville in Dallas County. Others of interest are Biscoe, Edmondson, and Thomasville in Arkansas; and Eatonville and New Monrovia in Florida. In Georgia are Archery in Sumter County, Burroughs in Chatham County, Cannonville in Troup County, Greenough in Mitchell County, and Leroy in Burke County. North Brentwood in Maryland deserves mention in passing, but more significant are Expose in Marion County, Renova, and Mound Bayou in Bolivar County, Mississippi. Oklahoma has the largest number of all. There are Boley, Bookertee, Clearview, Porter, Grayson, Langston, Lima, Mantu, Redbird, Rentiesville, Taft, Tatums, Tullahassee, and Vernon. Tennessee has Hortense in Dickerson County. Texas has one more than Alabama or Georgia. These consist of Andy in Cherokee County, Booker in Red River County, Oldham in Houston County, Roberts, and Union City. In Virginia there is Coardtown in Accomac County, and Hare Valley in Northampton County. School settlements, communities developed as the result of the establishment of large institutions, should be mentioned here. Such as Wilberforce in Ohio, Institute in West Virginia, Langston in Oklahoma, and Tuskegee Institute in Alabama make a favorable impression, but their opportunities are exceptional.

Some groupings in or near cities referred to as Negro towns are not really thus organized or con-

ducted. Most of them are so near the large cities
that in government, trade, transportation, and education they are under the control or influence of the
overshadowing urban centers. In most cases they are
natural suburbs settled by Negroes who transact practically all of their business in the cities. These are
such as Hobson City near Anniston, Mason City near
Birmingham, Alabama; Camp Nelson near George-

DR. U. S. WHARTON'S COUNTRY HOME AT HIGHLAND BEACH, MARYLAND

town, Kentucky; Lincoln, Maryland, near Washing-
ton, D. C.; Whitesboro near Cape May, New Jersey;
Columbia Heights near Winston-Salem, North Caro-
lina; Oberlin near Raleigh; Booker Washington
Heights near Columbia, South Carolina; New Bed-
ford near Chattanooga; Independence Heights near
Houston, Texas; Mill City near Dallas, in the same
State; and Ocean Grove, Titustown, and Truxton near
Norfolk, Virginia. The failures or successes of these

places should not be attributed to these Negroes living as such groups but rather to the aggregate of citizens living in these overshadowing cities and their vicinities.

Negro towns in the South have had a more substantial development than those of the North and West. Their population is not much larger but their life is more like that of a real town. They have had

HOME OF A PROSPEROUS FARMER

a more conducive surrounding population of their own race and have, therefore, been able to draw more from without than in the case of the Negro towns in the North and West. Buxton, Iowa, a mining town inhabited largely by Negroes, used to be referred to often in print, but on account of the exhaustion of the surrounding mines the town has ceased to be. While Brooklyn, Illinois, has a population as large as that of Boley, Oklahoma, the latter has accom-

plished so much more than the isolated town in Illinois.   Mound Bayou, Mississippi, with a much
smaller population than either has made a distinct
impression upon the country as an evidence of the
business acumen and enterprising possibilities of the
Negro.   The place is incorporated and well governed.
It has all the facilities of trade and commerce and
keeps in touch with the world.   There are small shops,
large grocery stores, general stores for all sorts of

A COMFORTABLE RESIDENCE IN A COUNTRY TOWN

merchandise, formerly a cotton mill, and still a bank.
Plateau, the town near Mobile, deserves special attention for the reason that it is composed largely of
Negroes who descended from the last cargo of slaves
brought to this country.   They came to Mobile in
1859.   Most of these people, therefore, are just one
or two generations removed from Africa.   Cudjo
Lewis, one of the slaves brought over in 1859, is still
living there (1929).   The business of the place is
largely controlled by whites, but the Negroes figure

in it sufficiently to make the situation an interesting study.

Most of these towns, unlike Plateau, however, are decidedly rural. They stand at the crossroads or near a railroad or navigable stream, at some point which did not formerly prove sufficiently attractive to white men in time for them to preëmpt it. As a rule, most of such vantage points are in control of the

THE STATION AT MOUND BAYOU, MISSISSIPPI

whites. They have taken their stand at the head of navigation and at the railroad center to avail themselves of every opportunity which nature or circumstance may offer. If in the miscalculation of things or as a result of lack of foresight some such place is missed, and Negroes come into possession of it, there is usually a way to dislodge them. The Negroes are generally offered what they originally paid for the site and urged to sell. If they refuse the blackhand society usually sends a Ku Klux notice that they must sell out and move; and if they still refuse they are harassed until they have to go. Sometimes when Negroes thus settled have permanently attached themselves to the community and have the respect and co-operation of the better class of whites they are supported in standing their ground and do not have to fear. It is seldom that the terrorizing element of whites constitute a majority of the community, but few white men are willing to champion the cause of the Negroes even when they know that they are being

RESIDENCE OF A NEGRO DENTIST IN A SMALL TOWN

persecuted. It is almost as unpopular to be a "nigger lover" as to be a "nigger."

There is not much of interest in these towns for the outsider. In most of them there are only a few comfortable homes, a small number of stores, a church or two, a school, and a post office. The population is not rich enough to afford taxes to lay out the place properly, pave the streets, and provide proper drainage and sanitation. In a town of white persons of the same size there would be an industry, a person, or

The Carnegie Library, Mound Bayou, Mississippi

Service Station, Mound Bayou, Mississippi

a few persons of sufficient wealth to afford all of
these things; but in the case of the Negroes they are
all poor alike and suffer together from cess pools,
contaminated water, and exposed food. On account
of these conditions the small town is better off than
the larger ones, because the dangers arising from

THE MOUND BAYOU OIL MILL   THE HOME OF THE LATE ISAIAH T.
      IN MISSISSIPPI   MONTGOMERY

these conditions would be less in the former. It is
not the Negro content with living such a life, but the
Negro forced by circumstances into a situation from
which his poverty will not permit him to extricate
himself. The Negro is blamed when he moves away
from such a town or settlement into a white community. His critics say that he is trying to be white
or he is running away from his people, but he is actually running away from death.

There might arise also the question as to why such Negro towns with so many disadvantages should survive. Sometimes such centers exist as such when there does not seem to be any independent economic basis to assure their future. To the perpetuity of these establishments, however, the social life of the place is a contributing factor. In these places the

A NEGRO RURAL HOME   A MOUND BAYOU ENTERPRISE

Negroes have more freedom than in towns with a preponderance of whites. The Negroes thus by themselves can work out their own affairs with so much more independence than in other communities. The entertainer can sing and play with spirit, the teacher can expound more profoundly, and the minister can preach without fear of molestation. What they do in such places is not so easily brought under the scrutiny of the other race, and unless something disastrous develops to disturb the peace of neighboring people these Negro townsmen move on in their own way.

In the rural South, too, the progress of the Negro is impeded by the limitations of the social contact of the races. Negroes may go to white stores for

SEVERAL SLAVE HUTS   CUDJO LEWIS

their supplies, but they must get their mail, buy what they want, and leave town unless there is a Negro quarter where they may lounge around; and even there strange Negroes must not tarry too long. Sitting around on the benches and empty boxes at country stores are usually a number of white men indulging in family gossip, discussing business, or debating political questions; but Negroes frequenting these places cannot take any part in such extra

RAILWAY STATION AT BOLEY, OKLAHOMA

THE HOME OF A WELL-TO-DO NEGRO

mural activities. Negroes are prohibited by custom from delving into the family secrets of the planter class; they are not supposed to understand business; and they are eliminated from politics. In this circle, then, they have no place. Negroes cannot participate freely in horse-trading on court days at the county seat of government, but if one of them has a fine animal which some white man wants, he is not above

ADVANCEMENT IN BEAUTIFYING THE SURROUNDINGS

making an effort to get it from the Negro, and he often succeeds in so doing.

In the more liberal parts of the Upper South these restrictions are not so rigidly enforced by the un-written law. But wherever Negroes are found in con-siderable numbers, they usually devise some scheme for frequent and close association among themselves to provide that social life which they do not enjoy as members of the whole body. This situation, then, accounts for a good many groupings of Negroes in settlements or communities which otherwise would have no other *raison d'être*. A much larger number of them would develop, and the Negroes in them would increase more rapidly if such centers had an economic foundation upon which they could build. As they

The Home of D. S. S. Goodloe, Near Bowie, Maryland

now stand a large number of them are dependent upon forces from without. These settlements and towns, therefore, have not increased in proportion to others or in proportion to the increase in the Negro population as a whole.

CHAPTER VII

RECREATION among Negroes in the rural districts is a problem. These people have such difficulty in making a living and must spend so much of their time in this important effort at self-preservation that little or no time is left for organized or directed recreation as it exists in urban centers. The working hours in the country are the longest of all in the laboring world. As a rule, a laborer rises at daybreak, is at his task at sunrise, and toils until dusk. Worn out at the end of the day, only the most robust have sufficient energy to spend a few hours of the night in seeking pleasure; and in the case of scattered population social functions are so far removed from the homes of those attending that it is still more taxing to go long distances before such wants can be supplied. The poor roads which until recently made travel most laborious added another difficulty to be overcome by seekers of pleasure.[1]

The moralist would say that these hindrances to worldly pleasure are a Godsend. Whereas the people in the city are more easily corrupted by accessible recreation of all sorts these influences are removed

[1] With very few exceptions these facts on recreation were obtained here and there in rural districts by observation of the five investigators of the Association for the Study of Negro Life and History. A number of these facts, of course, were taken from reports on recreation.

from the environment of the peasants. Experience, however, has shown that this is not true. The fact that places of amusement may be few or difficult of access often means that such opportunities as are allowed may be abused. A man who cannot often go to a resort may stay there too long or unduly indulge himself when the opportunity presents itself apparently once for all. Furthermore, in case such

A CROWD OF HANGERS-ON

resorts are few, he may have little choice as to the kind he may frequent; and he may more easily fall into the most undesirable company than he would in the city where a variety of amusements would be possible. In rural communities, too, the small number of persons qualified to participate in a desired amusement may be so few that well-disposed persons frequently learn to associate with those known to be far down. The less choice the greater the chances for evil influences.

The time allotted for amusements among Negroes

in the rural districts to-day does not differ much from what it was during the days of slavery. The economic system of the rural area is such that the Negroes are almost as hard pressed as they were when slaves. If the Negro laborer is working for wages he is not allowed to idle. He must work or quit; or he may be forced to stay on the job. In the case of most tenants, as shown above, the Negroes must often go and come according to the dictates of their landlord. The only time for play, then, is when they are not actually needed in the service of the planters. Inasmuch as the planters can always find something for their dependents to do, the play period is often reduced to the spare moments snatched from the overcrowded day, sometimes indulged in contrary to the will of the employer, and severely penalized when brought to his attention. Work, then, is for the Negro peasants while pleasure is reserved for their employers.

Nothing illustrates this attitude better than that one of the most alarming signs of the misuse of freedom, as the press of the planters saw it, was when in 1865 the freedmen in certain rural communities dared to stop work on special days to indulge in pleasures as the former ruling class had been long accustomed to do. These papers were daily filled with the most exaggerated accounts of such activities of Negroes. And in a sense it was truly alarming, for the plantation area was dependent on the labor of the Negroes. The whites would not work. Now if the Negroes also joined the leisure class the country would be ruined. By politics, economic pressure, and terrorism, therefore, the rural Negroes were quickly eliminated from the pleasure seeking class

and forced downward to such drudgery as they had
followed before the Civil War. The name of it was
different, but the situation was practically the same.
There were no special regulations as to the extent of
the diversion in which Negroes should indulge, but
public opinion soon brought it to pass that the will
of the planter class was generally respected, and

On the Way in Quest of Play

Negroes governed themselves accordingly as if by
an unwritten law.

With a limit set for leisure among rural people,
therefore, they have to indulge in only a few pleasures, in those requiring the least time from their work.
Diversion among people thus circumstanced, therefore, too often becomes licentious,—restricted largely
to drinking and sexual indulgence. It does not require very much time for a man to get a drink and

be happy with his dulcina. With the coming of pro-
hibition the use of strong drink has become more
expensive. The bootleggers in the rural districts,
however, ply their art without much restraint and
sometimes it is difficult to see very much change since
this experiment. White moonshiners preferably
serve Negroes because it is known that they are
afraid to disclose such operations. Among the rural
people to-day, therefore, there is found just as much
distilled liquor as was the case in former years, and
they boast of having it purer than the city "stuff"
because less interference with its manufacture enables
it to become well-seasoned.

Sexual indulgence is a popular recreation for most
rural people of both races. The pleasure-seeking
peasant finds such gratification under the cover of the
night, rejoices over the conquest, and returns in an
exhausted condition to work on a few days longer until there comes the impulse for another such thrill.
There are occasional visits of the mentally undeveloped pastor, but he is more concerned with emotion
than with thought, and his distracted, protracted
camp meeting effort is often followed by an increase
rather than a decrease in sexual indulgence. It is
not the fault of the minister,—not the fault of the
Church. It is the inevitable when people who have
such a little outlet are suddenly brought together in
considerable numbers. When amusement is not directed along sane lines it often develops spontane-
ously in the wrong direction. People are told that
they should practice self-restraint, but they are not
likely to do so without the necessary agencies to guide
them properly. In the rural districts, too, moral
teaching is too often negative. People are cautioned

not to do this and that, but the very persons thus
exhorting them are not prepared to assume the leadership in doing the many other things in which they
could harmlessly participate.   Such preachment is
tantamount to diagnosing a man's case as alarming
without prescribing a definite remedy for his recovery.

IMPORTED DIVERSION

Some of these present-day troubles have resulted
as a natural consequence of passing through a tran-
sition period.   The older forms of amusements are
almost out of date.   The people in the country no
longer find pleasure in them.   There has been so
much dissemination of information even by observation and contact that in spite of the illiteracy of
Negroes in the rural districts, they, too, are longing
for pleasures like those of the city.   They formerly

enjoyed the husking bee, the barn-raising, the quilt-
ing party, the harvest festival, the singing school,
the spelling match, hunting, fishing and the popular
picnic in the nearby woods. These things have been
replaced as a result of improved transportation
through good roads, by the radio, moving pictures,
and the like. "Let us have recreation like that in the

IN DOMESTIC SERVICE TO ASSIST   USING THE SPARE MOMENTS
OTHERS AT PLAY   PROFITABLY

city," they say. "Let it come from without rather
than as formerly from within."

An individual here and there, however, cannot furnish such facilities for recreation. It must be done
by coöperative effort of the community or by some
business man exploiting the public. As one has said,
"The rural picnic spot has been turned into a commercial amusement park; the sylvan retreat into the

private estate; the swimming place on the lake into the bathing beach; the fishing grounds into the private game reserve; the quiet lake with its rowing parties into the center for the private launch parties or public regattas. It is either 'no trespass here' or 'pay as you enter' there." [1] Urban recreation then, has become the dominant factor in rural recreation.

For the rural Negroes this looks disastrous. In their poverty they are unable to provide recreational facilities. They are left, therefore, practically without any such provision for play. While the rural whites are being supplied by the changed agencies the Negroes around are barred therefrom by race prejudice, and the community cannot afford a dual system of recreation when one is a heavy burden. Negroes are not admitted to the commercial amusement park, which has taken the place of the old picnic ground. They are turned away from the bathing beach which was once a free-for-all swimming place. There are very few places along the Atlantic ocean or the Gulf of Mexico where Negroes are allowed to plunge. Negroes are not admitted to the private game reserve which occupied the old fishing and hunting grounds, and they cannot have any parties on the placid lake where they once rowed their canoes without fear of disturbance. Some feeble efforts among the Negroes to provide such recreational facilities in imitation of the whites have resulted in more mockery than service. Their economic condition is such that adequate capital for these things cannot be spared from business channels, the needs of which are considered more urgent and important.

The more localized recreation also has tended to

1 C. J. Galpin, *Rural Life.*

pass away among the Negroes in the rural districts. Formerly a great deal of amusement was found in such as the "sugar stew" or "taffy pulling," the "pound party," marriage feasts, and festivals. These things give much less thrill now than formerly. The increasing interest in modern dancing has provided some outlet. Here and there is found a dance

READY FOR PLAY OR MISCHIEF   AN EXPERT IN DANCING

hall where people from around come in periodically for such diversion. A few decades ago the Negro Church was so militantly arrayed against dancing that this recreation had little chance to develop. In those days you could abstain from dancing and be saved, or dance and be damned. The changing attitude of the Church in our day, however, has been reflected in this case even in the country. The stage

dance, more difficult to arrange for than the private
dance, has tended to become less objectionable in
parts where public opinion once prohibited it.   Yet
this form is becoming too antiquated for the recreation required in imitation of what goes on in the city.

The rise of the automobile has tended to make the
recreation of the rural Negroes more dependent upon
that of the city than that of the whites. The Negroes
are not admitted to the rural amusement places which
have taken the place of those of old, but with good
roads and an automobile they can frequently visit the
city. There too often they come into contact with the
worst rather than the best. The Travelers' Aid Society is of little help to them, and the agencies to arrest the decline of those thrown into undesirable
groups seldom take Negroes into account. Furthermore, this quest for city pleasures is sometimes made
easy of satisfaction by the frequency of excursions to
large cities. Most of the persons in the South taking
advantage of these opportunities are Negroes. They
would naturally feel the need of it most, inasmuch
as they have such a little recreation at home and
cannot otherwise bear the expenses of going a long
distance. On Sundays and holidays excursion trains
bring them to urban centers in large numbers for the
joys of a single day. Endeavoring to divert themselves to the utmost in such a short time, they indulge in excesses which too often have disastrous
results. Conditions which are too frequently spoken
of as the results of traits in the Negro are actually
the results from other intolerable economic and social
conditions imposed by the very persons who make
such nonsensical remarks.

Most rural Negroes are not only prevented from

using the same recreational facilities as the whites, but they cannot otherwise and elsewhere indulge in amusements at the same time that the whites are thus engaged. Occupying the lowest status in the social and economic spheres, the Negroes must serve while the whites play. Recreation in the rural districts, then, is handicapped not only by the burden of dual

A BARBECUE

provision for such activities, but also by the double time required. After the whites have had their joyous time on various occasions, the Negroes who have served them during these days may have some time thereafter to divert themselves. The Monday following Easter and that following Whitsuntide are still observed in certain parts as holidays for the Negroes, who never think of this custom as a relic of slavery. Things must remain idle until pleasures have had their rounds before the situation becomes

normal in those parts. There is no reason why this
should be so. We are told that it is the custom of
the country, and that is considered sufficient explanation. In the more enlightened parts of these rural
districts, however, this custom has lost ground.

In what sort of recreation do these Negroes indulge? It would be most natural for them to imitate
their white neighbors. Their lower economic status,
however, sometimes makes this impossible. White
persons of considerable wealth may engage in amuse-

IN THE SURF

ments which are too expensive for Negroes—such as
the tournament, the chase, and the like. The Negroes
in certain parts where prosperity has favored them
have not delayed in going in the same direction,
though often with meager provisions. The large
majority of Negroes in the rural districts, however,
must remain content with those amusements which
are less expensive. In this respect they are on the
order of poor whites similarly circumstanced, but the
social aspirations and activities of these two classes
are not on the same level. The poor whites would
content themselves with the inexpensive pleasures

of the richer persons of their race. The Negroes would indulge in all of these and at the same time engage in others which do not appeal very strongly to the whites because of their rather cold and phlegmatic temperament in contradistinction to the exuberance, and vivacity, growing out of the emotional nature of the Negroes.

A detailed account of these social affairs of the rural Negroes would not differ materially from accounts of earlier observations of these people. As progress in these parts is rather slow things social have remained almost as of yore. While recent progress has put an end to most of old amusements, some of them have endured. There remain the marriage feast, the infairs, the taffy-pulling, the surprise party, the church suppers, and the private "break-down." With these one sees the old time excessive emotional outbursts as pent-up expressions will give rise to. While these amusements have resulted from the taking over of the culture of the whites the Negroes have added thereto a zest and enthusiastic expression which mark them as peculiar to the Negroes themselves. There is not a moment for sadness. No one frequents the place to brood over things. Dull care must be driven away. Rejoice and be glad. "Christmas comes but once a year, let us have a jolly time here." "Eat, drink, and be merry, for to-morrow we die."

Athletics, too, supply much recreation for the youth where religion has not put such under the ban. While city churches of Negroes are often the rallying point for such activities, the rural churches, still dominated by pioneer and conservative ministers, will not tolerate competitive athletics. If you shoot marbles, play croquet, or indulge in baseball your soul will be damned. You did not find Jesus by doing these things; you cannot reach the portals of glory by doing them. Even in the rural districts, however, there are a few young people who do not "give a damn if they are damned" because of athletics. Such bold recreation seekers organize athletic teams which

AT PLAY

by contests among various others in the district furnish considerable recreation during the late spring, the summer, and early fall. This is generally true in the more advanced sections where the employers are most liberal with respect to holidays and especially in the case of Saturday afternoons. The use of Sunday for such things is not popular even among those who are not religiously inclined. It just is not the custom. The boy who had his eye knocked out

while playing a game on Sunday is pointed out as a
warning to others not to tempt God.

Interest in athletics has tended to increase, but the
hard worked individual has no time to give thereto,
and how can he develop much interest in football or
baseball when at the close of his day's toil he is so
nearly exhausted that he must conserve his energy
for his task in the field the following day? The more

A MEETING OF A FARMERS' CLUB

advanced phases of athletics, therefore, cannot invade
the rural districts because of the very nature of
things. Most recreational activities, moreover, cannot be staged so easily as baseball which may be
set up fairly well with merely a ball and a bat. Indoor sports which require considerable outlay, of
course, are out of the question. In winter time or
during inclement weather, then, this sort of recreation is reduced to the lowest terms. The rural males,

then, must call at the firesides of the girls whom a few weeks earlier in the year they could take to an outdoor festival, a picnic, or barbecue in which athletics figured. Efforts are made, of course, to supply this remaining social need by increasing the number of indoor entertainments in proportion as the others pass out for the year. Attendance at such, however, does not equal that of the bright days of sunny summer unless they are so multiplied that persons would not have to go far for such diversion. Distant travel in the winter time for persons poorly clad, going and returning from such entertainments after heated exercises at dancing and the like, often results in large mortality from pulmonary diseases among Negroes in the backwoods of the Upper South.

In case of a rather free use of intoxicants disastrous results may result from these recreational activities. In one place a girl seized another and dispossessed her of her transformed hair because she stepped on the enraged one's white shoes. Elsewhere a boy cut another with a razor when he said disparagingly in the presence of some pretty girls that the slasher was not so good a man as he was. An unfortunate suitor struck his rival dead with a stone as soon as he appeared at a party with the girl who had rejected him. A husband shot another man dead on the spot for the reason that he danced too long with his wife and she seemed to enjoy the diversion. At one of their festivals a woman cleverly devised the sale of a special piece of poisoned cake by which she easily killed the drinking woman who had alienated the affections of her husband. In numerous cases whole parties broke up in uproarous rioting of cursing, slashing, and killing resulting in the deaths of several persons and the discomfiture of those held responsible for these infractions of the law.

CHAPTER VIII

THINGS OF THE SPIRIT

FROM the point of view of the Negro peasant things of the spirit constitute the most important concern of man. In the rural communities the pastor is still the outstanding man in the group in that he plays the important rôle of its spiritual adviser. He is regarded as the most honest, the most sincere, and the most devoted of those who toil among the lowly. This has changed somewhat in respect to the whites, but the rural Negroes, who because of custom and social and economic handicaps cannot develop any other professional class, must look to their clergy. The white neighbors of the rural Negroes are glad to have it so. Under almost any sort of pretext a Negro lawyer, physician, or dentist may be driven out of a rural community, if a few whites decide that he should go; but the Negro preacher is seldom disturbed, if he "sticks to the Bible." He is regarded as a factor in making the church a moral police force to compel obedience to what is known as moral obligations. He is also an asset in that he keeps Negroes thinking about the glorious time which they will have beyond this troublesome sphere and that enables them to forget their oppression here. White people, therefore, give more readily to religious work among the Negroes than to any other of their needs, although what they do give is inadequate.

149

With such an unusual advantage, then, the Negro rural church is in no sense decadent, as it sometimes seems in the case of the rural white churches. Statistics show encouraging progress, in numbers at least, from year to year. The rural Negroes maintain about three times as many churches as the urban Negroes do and the same proportion holds with respect to the Sunday schools. Most of these rural churches, of course, are found in the States below the Mason and Dixon line where the large majority of this element of population lives. According to the special *Census of Religious Bodies of 1926*, 88.7 per cent of the Negro churches are found in the South Atlantic and East South Central divisions. While most Negro churches in the North are found in cities, moreover, 84 per cent of the churches and 70 per cent of the members are rural in the South Atlantic and East South Central divisions. In the East North Central States 81.6 per cent of the Negro churches and 95.5 per cent of the membership are urban. Whereas the average membership of a Negro church in a city was largest (297) in the Middle Atlantic division and smallest (86) in the Mountain division, rural churches had the highest average memberships (104) in the South Atlantic division; those in the East South Central had 92, while the 27 Negro rural churches in the Mountain division and the 26 in the Pacific averaged respectively 41 and 35 members.

Negro churches, like the Sunday schools, were largely concentrated in the South, 32,332, or 88.9 per cent of the churches with schools, and 1,789,095 or 83.4 per cent of the scholars being located in the three southern divisions. Because Negro churches in the North are primarily urban while those in the South are mainly rural, it happened that the Negro Sunday schools with the largest memberships were found in the Middle Atlantic division, where the average was 107.9 scholars to a church. In the New England division this average was 99.7; in the East North Central area the number was only 47.1; and in the Mountain division only 40.5.

AT A COUNTRY CHURCH

The stability and progress of the rural Negro church is due to the fact that it is generally orthodox. The large majority of the Caucasians have abandoned real Christianity and treat it as reminiscence, but among them are still found a few of the orthodox who hope to see this religion preserved through the blindly faithful Negroes. And well might they think so, for the rural Negro churches exhibit practically none of the tendencies toward modernism. They are composed almost altogether of fundamentalists. A study

of the Negro rural churches by investigation and questionnaires filled out in communities in Virginia, North
Carolina, South Carolina, Alabama, Florida, Tennessee, and Kentucky in 1927 and 1928 supports this
conclusion.

The institution is preserved in its original state.
The rural Negroes hear of the strange doctrines, but
few are thereby moved. They laugh at those who
doubt the existence of an all-seeing Providence and
question the divinity of His Son. The Lord has de-
livered these Negroes from too many trials and tribu-
lations for them to doubt His power or His interest
in mankind. God is not held responsible for the
Negroes' being carried away captive to be the slaves
of white men; but He is given credit for delivering
them from bondage. God has nothing to do with their
long persecution and the intolerable conditions under
which they have to live, but great praise should be
given Him for permitting them to exist under the circumstances. The evils from which these Negroes suffer, they believe, resulted from the sins of their fore-
fathers and their own shortcomings, but as soon as
they can be purified in the fire of persecution necessary to burn away the dross, they will come into the
enjoyment of the privileges now monopolized by the
highly privileged race. The church and the mystic
spell under which the Negroes live, then, is a most
important part in their life in the rural community.

What, then, is this rural Negro church? It is the
simple Protestant faith, largely of Methodists and
Baptists, who, with the exception of the difference
of opinion on immersion are very much alike everywhere among Negroes. The large majority of
Negroes belong to these two sects, as the accompany-

TABLE IV.—LEADING DENOMINATIONS AMONG THE NEGRO CHURCHES, ACCORDING TO NUMBER OF CHURCHES AND CHURCH MEMBERS, RESPECTIVELY: 1926

STATE	CHURCHES			MEMBERS		
	State total	Leading denomination	Number of churches	State total	Leading denomination	Number of members
New York	352	Negro Baptists	111	114,543	Negro Baptists	46,823
New Jersey	412	Negro Baptists	159	71,221	Negro Baptists	41,129
Pennsylvania	706	Negro Baptists	303	177,532	Negro Baptists	100,202
Ohio	622	Negro Baptists	272	119,529	Negro Baptists	73,922
Indiana	326	Negro Baptists	161	49,704	Negro Baptists	30,388
Illinois	523	Negro Baptists	259	137,31	Negro Baptists	83,839
Michigan	186	Negro Baptists	81	46,231	Negro Baptists	24,883
Missouri	645	Negro Baptists	244	82,207	Negro Baptists	42,299
Kansas	328	Negro Baptists	136	28,292	Negro Baptists	15,243
Delaware	152	African Metho't Epis. Church	63	12,459	Methodist Episcopal Church	3,717
Maryland	654	Methodist Episcopal Church	370	97,025	Methodist Episcopal Church	35,272
District of Columbia	147	Negro Baptists	83	72,382	Negro Baptists	41,262
Virginia	2,255	Negro Baptists	1,610	378,742	Negro Baptists	316,095
West Virginia	480	Negro Baptists	299	32,754	Negro Baptists	24,166
North Carolina	3,203	Negro Baptists	1,316	431,333	Negro Baptists	206,807
South Carolina	2,838	Negro Baptists	1,364	405,614	Negro Baptists	235,224
Georgia	5,201	Negro Baptists	2,900	538,093	Negro Baptists	381,312
Florida	2,093	Negro Baptists	884	190,893	Negro Baptists	98,194
Kentucky	1,103	Negro Baptists	589	127,126	Negro Baptists	83,837
Tennessee	1,958	Negro Baptists	896	226,823	Negro Baptists	138,605
Alabama	4,284	Negro Baptists	2,415	557,231	Negro Baptists	364,565
Mississippi	4,034	Negro Baptists	2,314	348,525	Negro Baptists	226,989
Arkansas	2,411	Negro Baptists	1,375	201,240	Negro Baptists	134,720
Louisiana	2,077	Negro Baptists	1,311	248,797	Negro Baptists	132,743
Oklahoma	990	Negro Baptists	559	68,379	Negro Baptists	47,363
Texas	3,910	Negro Baptists	2,071	351,305	Negro Baptists	234,056
California	192	Negro Baptists	75	25,763	Negro Baptists	10,454

ing table will show. A few rural Negroes are members of sects known as the Christian and Missionary Alliance, the Christian Church, the Church of Holiness, the Church of God, and others of the holy order with varying names signifying practically the same creed and mode of worship. Most of the other Negroes found in rural churches are Evangelican Lutherans, Episcopalians, Congregationalists, and Disciples of Christ. With the exception of Maryland, Louisiana, and a few places along the Gulf of Mexico, rural Negroes know very little about the Catholic Church.

In their simple way the rustic people of color contend for the principles originally enunciated by the Protestant Church fathers. Christ came into the world to reveal God to man. He gave His life to save evildoers, who must die in their sins and be brought to life in Jesus, if they hope to escape the fire and brimstone of hell; and even after being thus born again they must be careful, for the devil is always busily planning to swerve the faithful from the way to glory. Thousands of snares may hang the feet, but none should hold them fast. Do right at all times, do not become frivolous, and take life too leisurely. Do not indulge in the modern dance, but keep up the buck and wing dance if in so performing you do not cross your feet. Quit playing cards, throw away your checker-board, give up croquet, shun baseball, or football, and never bet. If you do these things the devil will claim you finally as his own. You may take a little home-made wine, or persimmon beer; and you may occasionally take a mint-julep or a toddy on Sunday morning before you have family prayers, but you must be temperate. You must not become in-

toxicated.   Furthermore, never swear.   "Let your
communication be yea, yea, and no, no, for whatso-
ever cometh of more than these cometh of evil.''

The importance of such teaching is best appreciated
in understanding that the Negro Church, whether
rural or urban, is the only institution which the race
controls.   The whites being Occidental in contradistinction to the Negroes who are Oriental, do not understand this Oriental faith called Christianity and

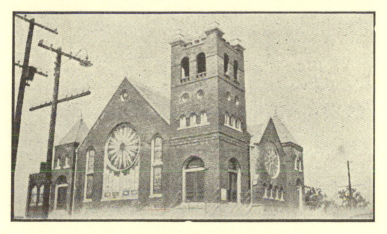

An African Methodist Episcopal Rural Church

consequently fail to appreciate the Negroes' concep-
tion of it. White people, therefore, have urged a sepa-
ration in church as in other things; and much more so
in the case of this than in other institutions: for, while
they separate the Negroes in education, recreation,
and the like, the whites, nevertheless, keep control of
these things. They make little effort, however, to
influence the Negro church. This institution, then,
has had the chance to develop in the way the Negroes
would have it. In their church they have more free-

dom than in any other sphere, and the Negro preacher among his own is in a class by himself.

Who, then, is this high priest in the rural community? He is not the man required to direct the religious work of an urban center, but "an inspired man" whom the fates have superimposed. He had a vision and he heard a voice which called him to preach.

GOING TO CHURCH

He had "to answer this divine call lest God might strike him dead." Such an inspired creature may have the rudiments of education or he may be illiterate; for in spite of his lack of mental development he can find a following sufficient to maintain a church. The Methodist conferences have done much to eliminate such clergy, but the Baptist conventions, although making a similar effort, have not yet succeeded. The Baptists enjoy so much democracy that they have no power to coerce the local churches. No Baptist church is subject to any authority but God, and sometimes it will disregard Him and run its affairs to suit itself.

As a rule, however, the Negro rural preachers are morally clean, much more so than those who labor in cities. There are certain shortcomings in all groups, but investigation has shown that the Negro rural priestcraft bears a good name. Their gravest fault is that they do not often pay their debts promptly. It seems that, having become accustomed to receiving things gratis, they cannot abandon the idea that in some way they can escape meeting such obligations. As a rule they will not lie or steal, and not many of them are found guilty of corrupting men's wives and daughters. In some communities where ministers have been found guilty of such things the whole class is given a very bad name for the offenses of one or two who happen to be exceptionally immoral. In this case all ministers are made responsible for the crimes of one, very much as a white community denounces all the Negroes as criminals when one of them happens to commit a dastardly crime. Of the thousands of questionnaires received and studied by the author only a few state that the reputation of the Negro rural preacher is bad, whereas in the case of cities this was often the comment.

What, then, is the preparation of the Negro rural ministers? For the special task in which they are engaged their formal preparation is practically blank. They do well to be able to read and write intelligibly. It may be that they have seen a few books on the rural church, but it is doubtful that they have enough mental development to understand them. Of late the white religious agencies are giving special training to ministers who will work among rural people.

From summer to summer now most of the sects hold special schools for Negro pastors for about four or six weeks, and some good has thereby been accomplished.[1] Negro rural churches, however, cannot draw freely upon such well prepared workers. At present there are only a few Negro youth aspiring to the ministry, and those, who do, go into the best churches in the cities. Because this condition obtains the ministry of the rural Negro church must be recruited from the mentally undeveloped members who have any amount of spirit but little understanding.[2] The rural church must take largely volunteer workers who cannot find opportunities elsewhere or who have other interests in the rural districts. While it must be admitted that by experience some of these rural ministers are better prepared than town preachers with a little more book learning, there is nothing in the average one of the group to indicate possibilities of leadership which the new program of the rural community requires.

The Negro rural church, therefore, has not made much progress beyond its status of reconstruction or antebellum days. Some Negroes in towns and cities enjoying contact with the outer world have remade their religion according to Caucasian requirements. The backwoods Negroes, however, have not been similarly moved. They see no need for changes in religion. Inasmuch as God changes not, and is just the same to-day as yesterday, how can a minister of

---

[1] Dr. James H. Dillard, of the John F. Slater Fund, and Bishop R. A. Carter, of the C. M. E. Church, have been very active in this work. Such conferences at Paine College, Hampton, and Tuskegee have been well attended.

[2] Immediately after the Civil War most educated Negroes went into the ministry. Now they go into other professions.

Jehovah advocate such innovations? "Give me, therefore, that old time religion," they say, "it's good enough for me." The rural Negro minister, then, will not proclaim a new thought. He will preach the same gospel in the same way. He has not changed and never intends to do so. "Others calling themselves ministers," he contends, "are bringing worldly things into the church; but as for me and my house we will serve the Lord."

On the Way Also

What, then, is this institution which the Negro rural minister directs? This question is difficult to answer, for while the outward appearances of the Negro rural church may seem like the urban, the two are inherently different. The urban church has become a sort of uplift agency; the rural church has remained a mystic shrine. While the urban church is often trying to make this a better world in which to live, the rural church is engaged in immediate preparation for the "beautiful land of by and by." The rural church building may be used for social uplift purposes, but this is not the church thus in action. These things originate without the spiritual group. When the rural church assembles in the spirit it is more of a séance. Persons have come together to wait upon the Lord. He promised to meet them there. They have no time for the problems of this life except to extricate themselves from the difficulties which will ever beset them here until that final day.

The worship of such an assembly is simple. There must be merely a reading of the scripture, singing, preaching, and praying. Then one must wait until the spirit moves him. The preacher makes his emotional appeal and the seekers within the courts respond with manifestations of the spirit resembling paroxysms which could hardly be expected outside of an insane asylum. With the spirits of the people thus fired up they can retire to their homes sufficiently uplifted to face the toils of another week or month. On assembling for similar services again they will have their spiritual strength renewed. This is the church visible and invisible. As such it considers itself the church militant, which, according to their faith, will some day be triumphant and take heaven by storm. "Sinner, you had better join the army before it is too late. Now is the accepted time."

The occasions for large accessions to the church, however, are not the regular preaching days or prayer meetings, for these are mainly to edify the elect. "To bring a large number into the fold" the rural churches hold camp meetings or protracted efforts. In July and August or at some other time when the peasants have harvested their crops they hold these revival assemblies. Food and money are more abundant at that time and the people are at leisure.

No two churches close together will have such a meeting at the same time. One takes up the first week of the month and another the second and so on to give the people of various communities the opportunity to follow these meetings from church to church. People from afar, who once came in carts and wagons, drawn by oxen and horses, may come to-day

A Rural Baptist Church   A Negro Rural Church

in automobiles. As the whole day for a week is taken up with services in the morning, afternoon, and evening, families must daily bring sufficient food for at least two meals. These feasts, then, are important functions of the assembly. The preachers must be fed, and sinners stricken with guilt must be cared for until "the Lord speaks peace to their souls."

There arrives, then, an abundance of nicely cooked vegetables, cakes, pastries, chickens, and watermelons galore. At noon everything is spread and made free. One may go from table to table and eat to his own satisfaction without price. Worldly people not the least interested in the religious effort often attend these meetings to feast and socialize with friends who are not otherwise brought together during the whole year. Men come to exchange news on the state of the community and to find out the prospects in various quarters. Girls expect to find there new fellows who may be attracted to them in gay summer attire. Young men similarly inclined come looking for new conquests. And with these are to be seen not a few widows and widowers bereft during the closing season but still believing that fortune may bring another companion with whom to continue on life's journey.

The seriousness of these people, however, does not permit the social to overshadow the spiritual. The minister and his visiting assistants are preaching three times a day on temperance, righteousness, and judgment to come. Prayers are offered hourly for those who are out of the "ark of safety." Repeatedly they sing such songs as

> *"Where are you going, sinner?*
> *Where are you going, I say?*
> *Going down to the river of Jordan*
> *And you can't cross there.*
>
> *"Oh you must have that true religion!*
> *You must have your soul converted!*
> *You must have that true religion!*
> *Or you can't cross there."*

The pleasure-seeking worldly persons, then, cannot long withstand this fervent appeal. Even the young ladies seeking beaux will refuse to socialize with sinners. "Before you talk love with me," one would say, "you must get your soul right with God."

Sinners, then, begin to weaken. They may stand up very well for the Sunday when the meeting opens and probably until Monday or Tuesday, but before the middle of the week you hear that some notorious person has been "convicted of his sins." This means that he has become thoroughly alarmed as to his lost condition and while in a state of prayer for deliverance from sin, he falls into a trance, prostrate like a man in dying condition. Friends come rushing up to minister unto his physical needs, trying to revive him. He gradually awakens from his stupor, praising God for pardoning him of his sins, usually saying with a peculiarly primitive intonation: "Thank God! Thank God! Thank God that I was born to die! He snatched me like a brand from eternal burning and saved me from hell's dark door. He said, 'O my little one, go in yonder world and tell both saints and sinners what a dear Savior you have found! I have plucked your feet out of the mire and the clay and placed them on the solid rock of ages where the wind may blow and the storm may rise but none shall frighten you from the shore!'"

This is what is considered a conversion. When noised abroad that a vile sinner has been thus saved his whole ilk and others of less crime become precipitously excited and readily answer the call to the anxious seat where they bow praying in the midst of sobs and tears, earnestly entreating the brethren "to take them to a throne of grace in their prayers."

Friends, especially interested in these sinners at the anxious seat, bow with them and whisper in their ears how "to find the way," while the minister vociferously contrasts the joys of heaven with the tortures of hell. Numbers of other sinners, then, become more easily "convicted," and soon they declare themselves "converted" and fill the woods around with outbursts of praise to God for what He has done for their souls. Before the end of the week, therefore, practically all malefactors in the neighborhood, except those commonly referred to as being "hardened in their sins," will be converted. At the end of the week the convocation closes with a sort of love feast, friends of the redeemed proclaiming more forcefully than the converts themselves their praise to God for "killing these people dead in their sins and bringing them to life in Jesus."

A few weeks thereafter comes the meeting when those proposed for membership in Baptist churches must demonstrate that they are actually converted and qualified for full privileges of the body. In the case of Methodists they must pass through a probation period. This is always easy, however, for all the candidate needs to do is to convince the brethren that he had some such experience as they themselves had—that he saw a light, heard a voice, had a vision, outwitted the devil, or received a visit from Jesus. With such a straight story they find ready acceptance in the church.

Most of these people, however, are frantically excited or "hell-scared." Yet, they go into the church with the intention to lead a better life. Having never thought the matter out carefully, however, and having never learned to practice restraint, many of them within a few months, easily go back into the life they formerly led; and the minister at his next revival meeting has to do his work over again. In all of these communities, then, one finds a number of persons who must "get religion" every summer because they "throw it away" during the winter social season.

Losing one's religion, too, is an easy matter in this Puritanic atmosphere; for you cannot sing worldly songs, cross your feet in dancing, play games, or go afishing on Sunday. Christ has called his people out from among the worldly. Yet if one indulges in these things only occasionally he merely backslides, and from him the right hand of fellowship must be withheld until, as a result of his prayers, the Lord condescends to heal his backsliding. Such a person, however, is often regarded as worse than a confirmed sinner, for "he that putteth his hands to the plow and then turns back is not fit for the kingdom."

CHAPTER IX

THE appeal of the Negro rural church, then, very much like that of the whites, is based upon fear. God is not so much the loving Father who has provided many good things for His obedient children; He is rather Jehovah, Lord of Hosts, working the destruction of those who do not heed His commands. This attitude is natural since this rural institution is without an educational program. The chief aim of the Church is to fire the communicants' emotion from time to time and to keep people sufficiently scared of evil by referring frequently to the horrors of the damned and the blessings of the "beautiful island of by and by." There may be a Sunday school, but this does not always follow the Church,[1] and the children attending it are presented catechism formulæ rather than an exposition of the Bible with respect to right living. The Sunday school, moreover, is not the nursery of the Church. It is conducted rather as a separate institution directed by workers who do not figure conspicuously in the work of the Church itself, and only a small number of persons attend it. Furthermore, you may learn all you can in the Sunday school, but you must still be "converted" before you are permitted to join the Church.

[1] The United States Census of Religious Bodies in 1926 shows that about six-sevenths of the Negro churches have Sunday schools.

Most evidences of progress are wanting in the Negro rural churches. A week-day religious school is out of the question, for very few Negro city churches provide such a department. The peasants have no such vision, and they are not so circumstanced as to finance a program of this kind. It is very seldom that there is a public lecture, for the people will not attend such an exercise. They prefer to hear a man speak to them "out of the mouth of

A CHURCH BY THE WAYSIDE

God." Very few of these rural people subscribe to religious papers, moreover, and those who do seldom read them. The Negro rural church, then, has no program except as it is expressed in the preaching service and the weekly prayer meeting. This institution is confined simply to the task of "saving and edifying souls." Circumstances which determine whether or not such souls may be saved receive little or no consideration. God will look out for these things if the people obey. "Serve the Lord," then, "and wait patiently upon Him, and He will bring it to pass." "You cannot by thinking add one cubit unto your stature. Stand, therefore, on the promises of the Lord."

The questionnaires returned showed practically no rural churches with a semblance of what is known to-day as religious education. Where actual teaching is the rule it is of the antiquated order devoted to the dissemination of Biblical truths and doctrinal matters which have no direct bearing on the development of the body and character of the individual. They teach subject matter but do not often "teach living spirit—to kindle interest, set free motives, stimulate thought, invite imagination, stir appreciation, whet curiosity, create ideals and lead them to find expression in action."[1] With the exception of the Sunday school, moreover, the young people's societies are not always active, and these may not continue throughout the year. Rural Sunday schools, too, are conducted mainly on the basis of the question and answer method with occasional exposition or lectures. What is taught is presented in a perfunctory manner and seldom influences the life of the child except when the repetition enables him to commit to memory certain facts which in later years he may accidentally learn the meaning of. Such methods as problem-project teaching, story telling, dramatization, instruction through manual activities and arts, or supervised discussion are hardly known in Negro rural churches.[2]

As a result, therefore, there is no direct influence upon the character of the people taught. They live

[1] Betts and Hawthorne, *Method in Teaching Religion*, p. 63.
[2] Hamilton and Garnett, *The Rôle of the Church in Rural Community Life in Virginia*, p. 66.

from year to year, attending church and Sunday school, but getting no new light on Christian living, inasmuch as the out-of-date ethical standards of centuries ago are still regarded as meeting the requirements of Christianity. The sick are neglected, the poor die in want, and must be buried in the potter's field; but these things are of little concern to persons who study the Bible from the medieval point of view. If a man is so improvident or unfortunate

AN UNUSUAL CHURCH FOR THE RURAL COMMUNITY

as to come to want, he must not expect others to supply his needs. Some may have that loving kindness and tender mercy to impel them to help such a dependent, but a man is not failing to perform his Christian duty if he takes no account of the indigent and wretched.

The frequent meetings of church bodies and societies in annual session do not adequately supply the much needed enlightenment as to the mission of man and his duty toward his fellow workers. Such

contact is helpful, but these assemblies assume too
often the atmosphere of vacation for the representatives assembled. They talk about difficulties rather
than take up such problems and solve them. The very
young people who should be helped by such conferences are seldom present and would not be very
much benefited thereby, even if they were, because
there are few practical applications of religion sug-
gested. Such immediate needs of the community as
better race relations, improved religious education,
and character building are generally neglected. Elo-
quent preaching and extraneous matters take up the
time of most of these bodies. Often, too, the question as to who shall be chairman of a certain com-
mittee, preside over a convocation, or direct a conference, assumes so much of a political aspect among
these rural people that their minds are not in condition to listen to or to carry out the sort of social
uplift program which the church actually needs. In
case of intense rivalries the large part of the time
may be consumed in the election of officers or in the
consideration of selfishly proposed resolutions to promote personal interests. This self-centered and conservative group, then, is still unable to see itself as
others see it. The institution is confining itself
largely to what has been and dreaming about what
will be.

With this restricted program, then, the Negro rural
church is doing little to save the youth from evils
which have crept in from the city. To enjoy a good
many harmless pleasures which the church would
deny them the youth have had to frequent the city
where they have learned at the same time to indulge
in other things which are harmful. If a young person,

then, cannot be scared into "saving his soul" he would not find it interesting to attend church except for social contact. That some young people do attend for this very reason is a cause of much complaint about the levity of the wayward youth. Having little or no interest in the religious exercises as conducted, they indulge too freely in whispering and giggling. Often when criticized for their attitude, the youth contemptuously laugh at the orthodox fathers and mothers who point out to them the dangers of the vengeance of God. Most rural ministers, therefore, consider the youth of to-day as belonging to the lost estate. "There is little hope for them and the world must be fast coming to an end if these are to be the men and women of to-morrow who will have to carry on the unfinished tasks of their fathers."

In urban centers special efforts have been made to make the church attractive to young people by giving their religious and literary societies much prominence and sometimes by maintaining what is known as the junior church.[1] The Negro rural church, however, as the questionnaires returned will show, makes very little provision for the youth. These young people must come into the church and conduct themselves in the old way or stay "out in the world with worldly things." The lack of talented persons to carry out such a program, moreover, is a serious handicap which this rural institution could not easily overcome even if it were alive to the situation. Persons with advanced ideas, too, do not easily find a following and,

[1] In the junior church the elderly people give up to the young for one or more Sundays a month all of the important positions in the church. The young people's choir sings, the notices are read by one of them, and still another prays and takes up the collection. This, however, is teaching the youth to imitate their elders, rather than to develop and carry out a new program.

therefore, tend to abandon the rural church to its fate rather than stay in it to reform it. Most Negro rural preachers are still skeptical about the religion of the educated classes, as hundreds of questionnaires filled out and returned attest.

In spite of an increase in numbers the Negro rural church during the last generation, therefore, has been losing ground to the rural school, of which we shall speak later. The building, being less frequented than formerly, does not get as much attention from the public. The people are learning to spend their money for other things to supply needs which the rural church does not consider. Those in charge of the Negro rural churches, however, never see these tendencies as resulting from any shortcomings of the institution, and about the only remedy applied is to censure the youth for a supposed change of attitude. The large majority of the questionnaires returned gave discouraging reports as to the attitude of the youth toward the church.

The failure to provide some of these things necessary for a new program, however, is due in a large measure to small revenue. It will be interesting, then, to inquire as to the support of the rural church. With a strong claim on the public as set forth above, one would expect the rural Negro church to be easily financed. Yet this is not the case. The income is usually meager merely because the members are generally poor, for Negroes give more to their churches than to any other institution as Table XIX, on pages 254 to 257, will show. Even when, according to the United States *Census of Religious Bodies in 1926,* we include the urban Negro churches, however, the average expenditures for each Negro church are low. In the seven States of Louisiana, Texas, Wyoming, South Carolina, Oklahoma, Arkansas, and Georgia they ranged from $800 to $600, while in Mississippi the average was only $476. Of the 39,245 Negro churches reporting their expenditures in 1926 the average for the whole country was only $561. The salary, when the rural congregation can offer one, then, is not sufficient to attract a well-prepared man. Many of these churches in these districts have done well when they raise two or three hundred dollars a year for this purpose. Some of them do not raise more than fifty or a hundred dollars.

In the remote districts, then, the average church cannot do better than to pay a minister for his service on one Sunday a month only. If the minister is fortunate enough to secure a church for each Sunday in the month, he may do as well on this circuit as one serving the same number of urban people every Sunday. In some respects he may be more fortunate in that he does not have to prepare a new sermon every week. A circuit is hard, but it is hard on the horse. The people thus served by a nonresident ministry, however, cannot advance rapidly. What they learn on the only Sunday of the month that services are held they forget or, because of insufficient stimulus, fail to carry out; and the minister on returning a month later must cover the same ground again. So many things which the minister is supposed to do for the community cannot be undertaken by a preacher who lives in a distant town and visits his congregation once a month to excite them for a collection.

The method of raising funds to meet such obligations varies. In many rural churches they do no more than to take up a collection after the sermon. In almost as many other cases the church gives some sort of entertainment the Saturday evening preceding the Sunday set for the services. These churches, as a rule, have not adopted the envelope system and they know practically nothing about that of the budget. The poverty of the members is such that it would be unwise to tax them. Few of the peasantry, moreover, would think well of the exclusion of members from the church because they cannot pay dues. Such a thing would seem un-Christian, for the poor are just as much entitled to salvation as the rich. They insist that salvation is free. They contend, moreover, that "if religion were anything which money could buy, the rich would live and the poor would die."

Fortunately or unfortunately, however, about the only obligation they have to meet is that of the pastor's salary, and if he is a real Christian he will not press the people too heavily for that. The services of the sexton or clerk are not expensive. The minister himself is sometimes one of the community, farming or working at some trade along with his parishioners while preaching as an avocation. This, of course, generally means poor pay for poor preaching. The services of most other officials working in the rural church are supposed to be given as a labor of love. Under such circumstances no one can be required to assume serious responsibilities and nothing of importance can thereby be accomplished.

For the construction of edifices the Negro rural church is often hard pressed in spite of the fact that they have more money invested in church property than any other institution. Many of their buildings

are never properly finished, and those which reach
that state soon fall into a dilapidated condition. In
the case of a shortage in the building fund the people
often contribute in kind. Some give labor and others
building materials. A whole community thus interested sometimes solves the problem much more
easily than those apparently better supplied with
cash. Many of these are crude looking log structures;
a larger number are frame buildings; but here and
there rises in the country a brick church which would
do credit to a city. One finds still, however, that the
average rural church is neither frequently painted
nor white-washed; its interior is not suitably dec-
orated; it is poorly lighted; and it is inadequately
heated. Few churches in these districts have any
such equipment as an organ or a piano. They maintain no playground. Athletics in which young people
are easily interested are not tolerated, because they
are too worldly to be brought into the church.

The poverty of the Negro churches, however, results
from their rapid multiplication. Over-churching is
one of the serious problems facing both the rural and
the urban Negroes. They split too quickly because of
ordinary strife among ministers and members of the
same sect, and they spend too much for unnecessary
structures to expand the work of ambitious denominations. While it is true that this work suffers
because these people lack adequate income, an increase in their earnings will not improve these
churches, if the money thus raised is to be unwisely
expended to satisfy sectarian bias. The Negro rural
churches need first consolidation. Some effort in
this direction is now being made, but abundant success is not in sight. Sectarian differences are too rife

to permit any such development as the interdenominational community church which is fast solving rural
religious problems. If the community has to support
a dual system of religion for two races, and then a
quadruple system for the work within each race, how
can the people rise with such a millstone around their
necks?

Of what assistance to the Negroes are the white
churches in the rural communities? Practically none
as an institution. As a rule the Negroes in matters
of religion are beneath the notice of the majority
of whites. In the first place, if the Negroes do not
have a church of their own in a community they
would seldom think of attending the white churches.
They would not be welcome there. The blacks and
the whites are serving the same God, but He has
not brought them to the position of worshiping Him
at the same altar. As a rule, a Negro minister would
not be tolerated for a moment in a white pulpit; but
occasionally an unusual Negro preacher may so favorably impress the public as to attract almost as
many whites as his own race. Frequently Negroes
welcome the ministers of these white churches. The
white minister, however, comes to speak in a patronizing fashion. "Now you people have been doing so
and so and you people must learn to do better."

In the same patronizing fashion, however, white
ministers and white churches in rural communities
have been of much assistance to Negro churches.
They have helped in building their edifices and in
defraying their expenses. Oftener, however, a
planter or contractor endeavoring to keep his Negro
laborers "satisfied," will build a church for them
and occasionally will contribute to the upkeep of the

pastor. In this case the employer of these Negroes acts selfishly in thus dictating the calling of a minister who will keep the people silent as to their unjust treatment. The Negro minister thus lacking moral stamina figures out a larger income from the rich employer than he can expect from his under-paid workers. Sometimes it becomes the fixed policy of such employers not to pay their Negro laborers money, for with it they might migrate; but they will-ingly provide for any such religious work for Ne-groes just as they often provide such a school as the segregation program of education in the belated parts will permit.

One cause for the lack of progress in all rural churches is that they have been neglected. There are religious education programs for these neglected people, but the superior denominational authorities do very little more for the rural church program than to deliver in *ex cathedra* form at religious con-ventions and conferences certain pronouncements as to what they feel should be done for the religious work among the peasants. Having directed little attention thereto, these dignitaries in giving advice sometimes do more harm than good. These officials, too, are generally uninformed as to the conditions in the outlying districts, and in the dictation of the program for such work they fail to take into account certain classes in urgent need of religious instruc-tion. The rural church, therefore, very much like the urban, tends too often toward the standard of the evangelical organization for the salvation and edi-mutual admiration religious body rather than an fication of all souls.

Unfortunately, too, the various programs for the

improvement of the rural church have not yet materially changed the aspect of those of the Negro institutions in the remote districts. The rural church program is somewhat new, and adequate funds for it have not yet been obtained. Not a few of the churches, therefore, must be neglected; and, of course, the Negroes are always the first to go lacking when all cannot be supplied. Some few of the agencies for the promoting of religious education are giving attention to the needs of the Negro rural churches, but they are handicapped by race hate, religious prejudice, or denominational bias. The so-called Christian white people in the communities where most Negroes are found will not take the Negroes wholly into their scheme of religious uplift for fear of too much social contact which might disturb the superiority of the Christian Caucasian.

Equally as much hindrance is found, too, among the Negroes, themselves, who are in many parts hopelessly divided along sectarian lines. The minister and his coworkers of the Baptist or Methodist faith will not readily coöperate with those who espouse the different creed. These two denominations have already preëmpted the field, and they do not care to give up their conquests. Other denominations at work among the Negroes often manifest more of a tendency toward coöperation, but they have such a little following that they do not make much impression in the backward districts.

The Negro rural church is undergoing change but not a revolution. While it is not to-day what it was a few years ago it is in spirit largely the same institution. In many parts of the South the population has been shifting from the rural districts to the

Southern cities and from the Southern cities to the industrial centers of the North and East, as reflected in the statistical tables herein given. It has been necessary, therefore, for a number of these churches to cease their operation because of the lack of sufficient members to support them. In some cases the pastors of these churches have gone with the people either into the near-by cities of the South or to urban centers to which they are going in the North. One of the chief causes for the lack of progress in the Negro rural church is that the young people especially, are leaving for the cities either for education or for industrial opportunities. As a rule they do not return; and, even if they do, their ideas are such that they are practically worthless in the support of the churches of their fathers. The Negro rural church seems to be helpless in having no program for meeting these exigencies. It must be approached from without.

The actual status of the Negro rural churches in comparison with the urban may be easily estimated from the statistics found in Tables XVI, XVII, XVIII and XIX on pages 242 to 257 in the Appendix. These give the details as to the number of church edifices and parsonages, the membership of both churches and Sunday schools, the value of the church property, the amount of money raised during 1926, and the debts of these establishments. Comparing these statistics with data published by the United States Bureau of the Census in 1906 and 1916, one finds that although the Negro rural churches have made some progress in material things, these institutions are still in a decidedly undeveloped state.

CHAPTER X

THE chief cause of the unfavorable conditions obtaining in the rural communities is that the people have not been enlightened, and the upper classes have not actually desired that their eyes be opened. Southern Negroes had their first chance at actual education upon the outbreak of the Civil War. Leaving the plantations from which they escaped for freedom, or because of being abandoned by their master's fleeing before the invading Union forces, Negroes crowded the army camps. The first effort toward the solution of this difficult problem of congestion was their education which was undertaken by officials of the United States Army. Following close upon the army teachers, came other forces offering a more thorough instruction through better organized schools. These organizations were largely sentimental and religious people who had sanguine expectations as to the coming of the Negroes into freedom. Long since restrained from participation in the uplift of these people, they now welcomed the opportunity to equip them for living on a higher plane and for occupying a more useful sphere.[1]

However great their enthusiasm might have been,

---

[1] Woodson, *The Negro in Our History*, 382-388; *Journal of Negro History*, VII, 1-40; IX, 322-345; XI, 379-415.

it was impossible to do for a large body of people what the state only can do. The United States Government, therefore, followed soon thereupon with the timely establishment of the Freedmen's Bureau which opened additional schools and systematized the effort. It was soon found impossible, however, to meet all demands with the limited resources on hand. The

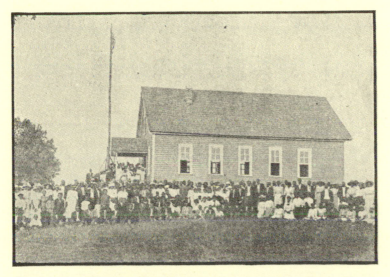

LOACHAPOKA SCHOOL, LEE COUNTY, ALABAMA, THE FIRST NEGRO RURAL SCHOOL AIDED BY MR. JULIUS ROSENWALD

inability and disinclination of the controlling classes of the Southern States to undertake a large part of this work made it impossible for these philanthropic agencies to accomplish as much as they had hoped. What educational facilities they afforded, therefore, were all that the Negroes enjoyed from the very beginning of this movement up to about the year 1870. By that time, about 10 per cent of the Negroes in need of education had been reached by the schools of the Freedmen's Bureau and the sectarian and non-sectarian associations engaged in the enterprise. Their illiteracy had been reduced to 79.9.

A turning point in the education of the Negro in the South was reached at that time as a result of political reconstruction. The Civil War worked the economic and social emancipation of both the poor whites and the Negroes. In spite of the strenuous

Mr. Julius Rosenwald, Mr. A. L. Smith, and Superintendent J. C. Lockhart, at the Zebulon School, Wake County, North Carolina, the First Brick Rosenwald School Which the Philanthropist Had Seen

efforts of the aristocracy to control these elements, as it did during the Civil War, a sufficient number of the poor whites, branded as scalawags, joined with the Negroes and interlopers from the North to force upon the South democratic education at public expense. The very proposal to tax the property of the state for the general uplift of the masses was scathingly denounced by the pulpit and the press of the

old régime as a violation of the sacred duty of the
state to protect the property of its citizens. Many
of this class feared that such an innovation would
result in the impoverishment of an already desolate
section laid waste by the ravages of a disastrous war.
It might also so inflate the cranium of the Negro
as to make him feel that he is as good as a white
man.[1]

The public school system was put in force, however, in spite of this opposition. It became so popular that some of the persons who had persistently
attacked the policy became its enthusiastic supporters
after it became known that the races would not be
educated together. Reduced to the extremity of hus-
banding all resources for the economic rehabilitation
of these states, however, public functionaries found
it impossible to make such a school levy as to provide adequately for an efficient dual school system.
Furthermore, sometimes in the hands of unsympa-
thetic officers, the school funds were diverted to other
purposes which their lack of foresight led them to
consider as more urgent needs. In this neglect of
the education of the masses, therefore, the Negro
schools suffered sometimes to the extent that a large
proportion of them had to be closed before they
could be permanently established. Inasmuch as the
States were too impoverished to provide one efficient
school system, it was impossible to maintain even a
makeshift system for the Negroes while providing
at the same time for the whites.[2]

[1] *The Journal of Negro History*, IX, 338-339; XI, 387-388.
[2] The situation is well set forth by R. R. Farr, the Superintendent of
Education in Virginia. The Negroes of that State, after waiting
patiently for years to reap the benefits of the public school system,
complained that although the ratio of the black and white population

From such a lack of provision for the education of the Negro masses, one may expect all sorts of concomitant evils. In the first place, school build- ings for Negroes were not established. Such schools as there were had to be conducted in rented homes, in lodge halls, in churches, or in abandoned huts. In 1910, 61 per cent of the Negro schools in Alabama were housed in such structures; 63 per cent in

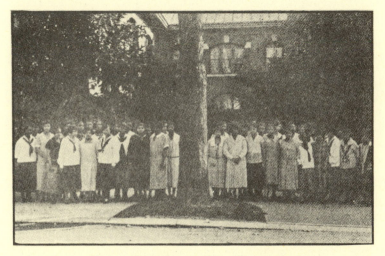

RURAL TEACHERS OF HOME ECONOMICS

Georgia, and practically all in Louisiana. In 1912, about 39 per cent of the Negro school houses in South Carolina were of this order. In the upper South in States like North Carolina, Kentucky, and

of the States was two to one, in favor of the whites, the schools es- tablished for the two races were in a proportion of three to one. Farr bluntly said, "The great discrepancy between the per cent of white and colored enrollment is readily accounted for. Because the whites have been provided with a fair proportion of schools to their school population, the blacks have not." See first report of R. R. Farr as State Superintendent of Public Instruction in Virginia, pages 58-59.

Missouri, only a small number of such structures were thus rented. These buildings in the neglected parts, as a rule, were uncomfortable, and if once all right, were easily allowed to go to ruin. The structures were made of logs or upright boards with such large cracks between them that the rain, snow, and wind played their part in contributing to the infelicitous condition under which these children had

TRAINING SCHOOL TEACHERS OF BERWYN, OKLAHOMA

to be taught. Furniture and equipment were practically nonexistent. There was little effort to beautify the exterior of the buildings or to take care of the grounds. In some cases, both the buildings and the grounds were untidy and filthy.

Under such conditions, a large percentage of Negro children did not attend school. The problem of attendance in Negro schools, moreover, tended to become more serious. In 1910, only about 60 per cent

SIX-TEACHER ROSENWALD SCHOOL, LAKE CITY, FLORENCE COUNTY, SOUTH CAROLINA

CALVERT SCHOOL, ROBERTSON COUNTY, TEXAS

of the Negro children between six and fourteen in
sixteen Southern States attended school. In some
of the Southern States, the percentage ran almost
as low as one-third; whereas in others, as in the
case of Oklahoma, Kentucky, North Carolina, and
Missouri, the per cent was considerably higher. The
attendance, too, was made still more problematic
because of the scattered Negro population. Schools
were far apart, and the Negro children sometimes

A Six-Teacher School with Vocational Room, Library and
Auditorium at Edgefield, South Carolina

had to walk more than five miles over bad roads to
attend school. In many parts of the South, these
conditions still obtain. Where there have been provided consolidated schools, the boards of education
pay the expense of transportation for the whites, but
in most cases the Negro pupils must walk.

The hopeless condition of these schools is further
shown by the inefficient type of teacher attracted

thereto.   Negro teachers well equipped for their work, found their way into the districts of the border States where better provision was made for Negro education with longer terms and higher salaries.   Up to 1910, the school term for Negroes in Alabama, Florida, Louisiana, North Carolina, and South Carolina was less than five months.   In Georgia, Arkansas and Tennessee it was from five to six months, and

COUNTY TRAINING SCHOOL, NEWTON, MISSISSIPPI

in Oklahoma, Kentucky, Texas, and Virginia, it was a little more than six months.   In 1910, the average annual salary paid a Negro teacher in Alabama was $158.87; in Florida, $186.70; in Georgia, $119.35; in Kentucky, $310.05; in Louisiana, $159.89; in North Carolina, $118.59; in South Carolina, $110.54 and in Virginia, $172.63.

Most of these teachers, too, had not mastered even the fundamentals.   The majority of them had not

even a sixth grade education. They could scarcely
write a letter or utter intelligently a few simple sen-
tences of the English language. They undertook to
instruct in the most elementary subjects and could
not do that successfully. Hundreds of letters obtained by investigators from such teachers in these
belated districts show what meager preparation they
had undergone before beginning their work.

Teachers of this type, however, were sometimes

RESULTS FROM REALISTIC TEACHING

preferred to those better trained, especially if they
had come under the influence of the schools established and maintained by Northern philanthropy.
Often the main point in the employment of a teacher
in a Southern Negro school was to place in the position some one who would maintain the point of view
of the whites of that district. The ability to teach
was not always the determining factor in the selec-
tion of a teacher. Appointment was often made without proper certification. A Negro woman cooking for

an influential white gentleman could usually have him secure the appointment of her son or daughter whether the applicant was competent or not.

Some little hope for the Negro peasantry, however, remained in the consideration given the needs of the masses by schools devoted to practical education. Carrying education to the class of Negroes still farther down, came Hampton and Tuskegee. The programs of these schools are to-day endorsed largely by

ELIZABETH CITY COUNTY TRAINING SCHOOL, VIRGINIA

the white people throughout the South because of their optimistic utilitarian program. Hampton was a New England institution established in Virginia for the education of Negroes. Out of it came Booker T. Washington, who owed his education to this school and to Wayland Seminary in Washington, D. C., an institution merged later with Richmond Theological Seminary to form Virginia Union University. While the point of view in Hampton and Tuskegee differed from that of the idealists promoting the Negro colleges and universities of the South, the two worked out in the end with the same result. The Negro was to be taught to connect his education with every-day life, to prepare himself to function in the environment in which he lives rather than to extricate himself therefrom for experimental transplantation to a different atmosphere. This industrial program began with the lower stratum as the foundation of all civic efforts intended to redound to the good of the whole community. It was impossible to carry the fortunate few of the Negroes to that degree of achievement to which they aspired without having as a basis for such structure, a more enlightened and progressive peasantry.

At the same time the industrial education policy, too, was diplomatic. It was engineered so as not to ruffle the feelings of the South. The whites might go forward with their system of education as they understood it. The Negroes were to be taught to serve and to serve efficiently. This program of optimism was deemed timely and gradually grew upon the Southern mind as a safe means by which the education of the Negroes might be encouraged without apparently offering them the same opportunities given the whites. In the wisdom of the expounders of this idea, however, they were actually offering the Negroes a system of education better than that provided for the whites, but only a few enterprising Negroes could be trained in these institutions of the new thought.

The crying need of the rural schools, however, had been deeply impressed upon the mind of an educator who had always worked to the end of uplifting the man farthest down. This man was Booker T. Washington.[1] How this emergency could be met seemed a far distant prospect. Fortunately, however, by the helpful contact of Julius Rosenwald with Booker T. Washington, a solution of this problem was eventually worked out. Mr. Rosenwald had otherwise manifested interest in the Negro and had found his philanthropy well placed. In the meanwhile, Mr. Rosenwald

VOCATIONAL BUILDING OF WILSON SCHOOL, IN ARKANSAS, WITH MR. W. B. HARRELL, SECRETARY OF THE JULIUS ROSENWALD FUND IN FRONT

was learning the story of Tuskegee and increasing his interest in the Negro.[2] In one of the earliest conversations with Mr. Rosenwald, Dr. Washington expressed his interest in the construction of rural schools for Negroes, a project in which others had

[1] There are several claimants to the honor of suggesting the construction of rural schoolhouses for Negroes. Perhaps, like many other movements in history, the idea was in the air and several workers got it at approximately the same time.

[2] The data herein given were taken from the files of the Julius Rosenwald Fund.

materially expressed interest but for which more
systematic support was required. Mr. Rosenwald
was finally won to the project. He said, ''I was willing to join Dr. Washington in a campaign for better
rural schools. I make it a condition that in these
campaigns, white and colored people must be interested, and that some of the money for these schools
must come from the white people; because where peo-

PUPILS OF A RURAL SCHOOL

ple work in a common cause, they learn to know one
another and to get along together.'' [1]

Six rural schools in Alabama communities were
first assisted. This experiment was conducted under
the Extension Department of Tuskegee Institute in
1913. To accomplish so much, however, was not an
easy task. Difficulties of travel, apathy, conserva-
tism, and religious antagonism beset these workers

[1] This statement is given in an unpublished account of the Rosenwald
Rural Schools.

in the beginning of this important effort. An epoch was reached in the development of the rural schools, however, when in 1914, Mr. Rosenwald promised to contribute an amount not to exceed $30,000 toward the cost of building 100 rural schoolhouses. Showing increased interest in this work of the rural schools and at the same time expressing appreciation for it, Mr. Rosenwald further encouraged Mr. Washington. In February, 1915, Mr. Rosenwald assured the educator that the money would be forthcoming for 100 more schoolhouses if it seemed to be the desirable thing to do when the first 100 had been completed.

The administration of the construction of the Julius Rosenwald Schools continued at Tuskegee after the death of Mr. Washington in 1915. There followed a greatly increased number of schools constructed, much enthusiasm in the extension of the system, and more highly favorable results obtained from year to year under the direction of Mr. C. J. Calloway, the head of the Extension Department of Tuskegee. As this division was not designed as an agency for such an undertaking, however, it was soon overtaxed by administrative problems when the movement had spread so rapidly as to cover a large portion of Alabama and parts of as many as ten States of the South. It was, therefore, decided to establish a central administration at Nashville, Tennessee, under the direction of Mr. S. L. Smith. The Julius Rosenwald Fund was duly incorporated, and the work was more thoroughly systematized. The General Education Board and the Jeanes and Slater Funds gave their support in providing for teacher training and supervision by special instructors. The State Departments of Education and local authorities worked in harmony with the school building officials and the rural school agents appointed to expand and extend the work. For a number of years Dr. F. W. Shepardson was secretary and acting director of the Fund until it was recently expanded and reorganized under the direction of Mr. Alfred K. Stern and the presidency of Mr. Edwin R. Embree.

DOMESTIC ART IN A RURAL SCHOOL

Difficulties in promoting the Rosenwald rural school development, however, made the effort more arduous than that of supplying a general demand. In the first place, it was not easy to interest the Negroes who were to be the chief beneficiaries of the system. They had long been duped and exploited by ill-designing persons who had come with plausible stories as to interest in their welfare. The Negroes did not have the confidence in themselves to believe that they could do such a thing and they were reluctant to think that persons far away, and especially those of another race, had so seriously thought of their condition as to bring them this unusual stimulus of education. When asked to raise a specified sum of money to profit by this proffered philanthropy, they still had doubt that their contribution would be matched by the philanthropist far away. Furthermore, when requested to purchase land and deed it

THE DEDICATION OF A DORMITORY OF THE SHELBY COUNTY TRAINING SCHOOL IN TENNESSEE

to the state for the erection of school buildings thereon, leaders in the communities often blocked the movement by pointing out the danger of transferring their land to the state.

On the side of the white people, it was equally difficult to arouse some of them in behalf of the Negroes, especially when approached by an outside agency. They had never seriously thought of education for Negroes as it had been provided for whites. The so-called educated Negroes, of course, had no status among them. Even when presented in the form of training the Negroes to be useful to the community, the whites could not understand why they should be asked to assist in building for Negroes schoolhouses which were more comfortable than those which had hitherto been erected for the whites. This was an innovation that few would willingly accept.

It was unwise, then, to impose such a program upon

THE SCHOOL, THE SHOP, AND THE FARM, MILAN, TENNESSEE

the community until at least an enthusiastic minority could grasp the new ideas of democratic education. To ignore these antagonisms, then, might result not only in impeding the progress of the work, but in the burning of the schoolhouses after they had been constructed. The rapidly increasing popularity of the rural school development, however, rendered the number of cases of incendiarism much less than was expected. The Rosenwald Schools, coming as an innovation, and worked out as a benefaction in the life

JASPER COUNTY TRAINING SCHOOL, GEORGIA

A THREE-TEACHER CONSOLIDATED ROSENWALD SCHOOL

of the Negro people of the South, moreover, effected tremendous changes through the coöperation of the two races. Negroes learned to work together and whites worked with them. The thing was done, and the liberal parts of the South became dotted with 4,464 schoolhouses, as the accompanying map so graphically illustrates.

The beneficent effects of this rural school construc-

LANCASTER COUNTY TRAINING SCHOOL, SOUTH CAROLINA

tion have been briefly summarized as improving the communities from the social, economic, religious, and especially from the interracial point of view. In the first place, the schoolhouse, often the most attractive public building in the district, became a social center for the Negroes and increased in appreciation from year to year. There followed, also, the remodeling of churches, the diminution of sectarian strife, more comfortable homes, improvements in sanitation, and changes in style of dress. Then came, too, the extension of the school term, increased attendance, higher standards among the teachers evidenced by more extensive preparation, the development of the feeling of dignity and responsibility on the part of the Negroes, and the diminution of the feeling of unrest among them. These schools coöperated effectively with the Home Administration Agents operating from the State Departments of Education with the support of

BOLIVAR COUNTY TRAINING SCHOOL, MISSISSIPPI

the Jeanes and Slater Funds and the General Education Board.

In estimating the beneficent effects of the Julius Rosenwald rural school construction, doubtless the most important of all was that of the development of self-help in the Negro. The institution of slavery unfortunately encouraged in the slave the tendency to be dependent upon a superior. In the early years of freedom, the property-less Negro turned loose upon the world to shift for himself invited the sympathy and benevolence of persons from without to the extent that self-help had little chance for development. Since the Reconstruction period, however, a few Negroes have economically advanced much more rapidly toward self-sufficiency, although the large majority of the race find themselves far from this point. It was most opportune that at this very time there came the plan for the construction of rural schools based upon self-help. Every Negro then had a chance to do what he could.

Informed that they could profit by this philanthropy only to the extent that they were willing to make some sacrifice themselves, not a few Negroes first regarded compliance with such terms an impossibility. When it had been actually demonstrated in various parts of the country that these schoolhouses could be built by a little sacrifice on the part of all, however, there was engendered the spirit of self-confidence and the tendency to rely upon their own initiative in doing their part in carrying out this progressive program. This element of self-help, too, is to be estimated not only on the basis of the assistance it has been in the construction of rural schools, but in the general uplift of the Negroes through other agencies which since then they have warmly supported.

A more striking result of the Julius Rosenwald rural school construction was the effect that it had on the whites. The schools thus constructed for Negroes were in many cases superior to those for the whites. In some instances, moreover, before there could be erected a comfortable schoolhouse for Negroes, one equally as good or better had to be built for the whites. In the communities where there was less racial strife and the Negro building was first constructed there was set going almost immediately an effort to establish a modern schoolhouse for the whites. In some instances, moreover, the Negro building was taken as a model for the building of the white school. The whites, of course, had no particular desire to be following in the movement in behalf of the Negroes, but the Rosenwald buildings were carefully worked out by architectural assistance and in accordance with the requirements of school hygiene. As most of the state departments had no special law providing for school construction they had made no such provision. Lacking funds to employ agents and architects for the supervision and the construction of such work, moreover, they found the best solution of their problems in following the plans already brought into the states by the Julius Rosenwald agents.

CHAPTER XI

STUDYING this rural school development which has been so extensively praised by the persons acquainted with this program and the efficient manner in which it has been carried out, one may get the wrong impression. While the results obtained in the use of the Rosenwald Fund have been unprecedented in the development of education in the South, it must not be thought that the whole task of the enlightenment of the Negro has been completed. There was so much to be done in the beginning and so many obstacles to be overcome before the work could be successfully prosecuted that what has been accomplished can be properly evaluated only by bearing in mind the neglected condition of the Negro peasantry when this movement was started. As a matter of fact, in spite of this extensive building program and the increasing interest in the development of the Negro schools established in the buildings thus made available, only about one-half of the Negroes in most of the Southern States have been actually offered real facilities of education. Where the South has been able it has too often been unwilling, and where it has been willing it has too often been unable. Considering the number of Negro children in the country and the number enrolled as set forth

[1] These data were compiled by Mr. S. L. Smith, the director of the Julius Rosenwald Fund, Nashville, Tennessee.

in the following summaries, one can more readily grasp the situation.[1]

The number of Rosenwald schools completed to July 1, 1929, was 4,464, costing $23,182,238, the teacher capacity being 12,594, and the pupil capacity 566,730. These schools have grown at the average rate of four classrooms for every working day from July 1, 1920, to July 1, 1929, providing modern school accommodations for one new pupil every three minutes of this nine year period.

"The Negro scholastics (children of school age) in the fourteen Southern States was 3,052,613, July 1, 1928, and 3,041,447 July 1, 1927, showing a gain of 11,066 or .3 of 1 per cent. There was a slight loss in the number of rural children but a gain in the cities and towns. Although all census reports show a decline in the relative Negro population in every Southern State except Oklahoma for the last two decades and an actual decrease in more than three-fifths of the counties, there was an unexplainable increase in the number of Negro children of school age from July 1, 1927, to July 1, 1928, according to State reports.

"The pupil capacity of the 4,464 Rosenwald schools (566,730) completed to July 1, 1929, was sufficient to

1 "Each year for the past three," says Mr. Smith, "a brief statistical survey of Negro schools in the fourteen Southern States has been made, securing information from State officials on (1) the number of schools, (2) the scholastics, (3) the enrollment, (4) the teachers employed, (5) the length of term, and (6) the value of school property. These data have been brought up to date, using the latest statistics available in each of the State Departments, as of June 30, 1928.

"The main purpose of this study has been to procure reasonably accurate data with which to make some comparisons of the Rosenwald schools on (1) the number of buildings, (2) the pupil capacity, (3) the teacher capacity, (4) the length of term, (5) costs, etc."

take care of 26.4 per cent of all rural Negro scholastics, a gain of 3.0 per cent over the previous year
(23.4 per cent). At this average rate of gain it would
require 8 years for the pupil capacity of the Rosenwald schools to equal 50.0 per cent of the scholastics
(if the number should remain about the same). But
since not more than 85 per cent may be counted on

DUNBAR HIGH SCHOOL, FORT MYERS, FLORIDA

to attend school this time might be reduced to 7 years.
At this rate it would require an average of almost a
quarter of a century to build enough Rosenwald
schools to accommodate all Negro children. Tennessee has just passed the halfway mark, while Oklahoma, North Carolina and Kentucky are between 40.0
and 50.0 per cent. At their present rates they would
be able to reach the saturation point long before Alabama or Georgia could provide Rosenwald schools for
one-third of their scholastics.

TABLE V—NEGRO SCHOLASTICS AND ENROLLMENT—RURAL AND URBAN
—IN 14 SOUTHERN STATES, 1927-28.

State		Scholastics			Enrollment	
	Total	Rural	Urban	Total	Rural	Urban
Ala.	327,563	250,612	76,951	182,082	140,097	41,985
Ark.	156,785	106,785	50,000	113,317	70,500	42,817
Fla.	141,954	87,230	54,724	93,539	56,600	36,939
Ga.	346,963	267,163	79,800	241,498	180,825	60,673
Ky.	56,749	29,574	27,175	48,272	26,427	21,845
La.	255,740	175,706	80,034	145,833	91,634	54,199
Md.	68,949	40,049	28,900	49,903	29,244	20,659
Miss. ...	464,748	374,258	90,490	274,932	226,575	48,357
N. C. ...	312,412	232,702	79,710	262,081	196,041	66,040
Okla. ...	53,922	31,000	22,922	49,301	29,610	19,691
S. C. ...	300,000	200,000	100,000	228,003	166,946	61,057
Tenn. ...	120,894	78,460	42,434	115,839	72,444	43,395
Tex.	229,032	103,640	125,392	201,315	94,081	107,234
Va.	216,802	170,835	45,967	152,293	114,046	38,247
Total	3,052,513	2,148,014	904,499	2,158,208	1,495,070	663,138
1926-27	3,041,447	2,151,018	890,429	2,105,929	1,457,495	648,434

TABLE VI—NEGRO RURAL SCHOLASTICS 1927-28 SHOWING WHAT PER
CENT THE TEACHER CAPACITY OF THE ROSENWALD SCHOOLS WAS
OF THE TOTAL SCHOLASTICS FOR THE YEARS ENDING JULY 1, 1929
AND JULY 1, 1928.

State	Rural Scholastics	Pupil Capacity	Rosenwald Schools Per Cent of Scholastics	
			July 1, 1929	July 1, 1928
Ala.	250,612	36,450	14.5	13.5
Ark.	106,785	39,015	36.7	31.0
Fla.	87,230	17,685	20.2	12.1
Ga.	267,163 #	30,150	11.2	9.1
Ky.	30,378	12,735	41.9	36.1
La.	175,706	47,520	27.0	25.8
Md.	40,049	11,925	29.7	27.3
Miss.	374,258 #	68,670	18.3	17.3
N. C.	232,702	102,150	43.9	40.3
Okla.	31,000 #	15,210	49.6	45.0
S. C.	200,000	65,565	32.3	30.7
Tenn.	78,460	39,780	50.7	47.3
Tex.	103,640	42,840	39.5	35.5
Va.	170,835	37,035	21.6	20.5
Totals	2,143,781	566,730	26.4	23.4

Decrease.

"The total enrollment in the 22,949 rural Negro schools for the year ending June 30, 1928, was 1,495,070, an average of 65 per school. The increase in rural enrollment in 1927-28 over 1926-27 was 37,575, or 2.5 per cent, even though there was a slight decrease in the number of rural children of school age. The per cent of all Negro scholastics enrolled in 1927-28 was 70.7—rural 69.7 per cent and urban 73.0 per cent—compared with 69.2 per cent in 1926-27.

"COMPLETE CONSOLIDATION"

Oklahoma leads in enrollment with 95.5 per cent, Tennessee follows with 92.3, Texas comes third with 90.7.

"The enrollment in Negro schools for the year 1927-28 was 52,929 more than for 1926-27, the increase in the rural schools being .5 to 1 per cent more than in city schools. Some of the state officials give credit to the Rosenwald schools for stimulating in part this increase in rural schools.

"While the average enrollment of Negro pupils in all rural Negro schools was only 65 according to last reports, the average pupil capacity of the 4,464 Rosenwald schools completed to July 1, 1929, was 129, and the previous year 124.

"The pupil capacity of the Rosenwald schools is sufficient to take care of 37.9 per cent of all rural Negro pupils enrolled. This is an increase of 10.5 per cent in two years. Although there was an enrollment increase in rural schools of 2.7 per cent in 1927-28 over 1926-27, the rate of increase in Rosen-

TRANSPORTATION BUSSES OF THE ROSENWALD SCHOOLS

wald schools capacity in 1928-29 was 2.9 per cent greater than in the previous year, Arkansas leading (61.4), Tennessee coming second (54.6), and North Carolina third (52.1). Georgia still holds the bottom place (16.6) while Alabama (26.0) was forced from third to second place from the bottom by Florida (31.7).

"Since the enrollment may be expected to increase with better schoolhouses, trained teachers, health conditions, bus transportation, a greater fervor of spirit, it is difficult to say just how long it would take at the present rate to build enough Rosenwald schools to house an average of 50.0 per cent of all the rural Negro pupils enrolled. Tennessee, North Carolina, Louisiana, and Oklahoma have already passed 50.0 per cent, and Arkansas has passed 60 per cent, and they are making satisfactory annual increases, the rate of Arkansas being more than 8.0 per cent for each of the past two years.

"As more attention is given to the qualitative along with the quantitative, the teacher load will be reduced, requiring more classrooms for a given number of pupils, and special high school facilities will have to be provided to take care of the rapidly increasing number of high school pupils. This is explained by the accompanying tables of data by states.

TABLE VII—NEGRO RURAL ENROLLMENT BY STATES 1927-28 SHOWING WHAT PER CENT THE PUPIL CAPACITY OF THE ROSENWALD SCHOOLS BEARS TO THE TOTAL ENROLLMENT.

State	Rural Enrollment			Rosenwald School		
	Number	Per Cent of Scholastics	Pupil Capacity	Per Cent of Enrollment		
				7/1/29	7/1/28	7/1/27
Ala.	140,097	55.5	36.460	26.0	24.2	20.7
Ark.	70,500	66.0	39,015	61.4	53.5	43.7
Fla.	56,600	64.8	17,685	31.7	20.3	11.3
Ga.	180,825	52.1	30,150	16.6	14.3	12.0
Ky.	29,214	89.3	12,735	43.5	36.9	28.5
La.	91,634	52.2	47,520	51.8	50.0	35.1
Md.	26,427	73.0	11,925	40.7	37.3	28.7
Miss.	226,575	60.5	68,670	30.0	29.7	24.3
N. C.	196,041	84.2	102,150	52.1	48.9	37.6
Okla.	29,610	95.5	15,210	51.3	50.7	36.8
S. C.	166,946	83.4	65,565	39.2	40.0	31.4
Tenn.	72,444	92.3	39,780	54.6	50.6	41.0
Tex.	94,081	90.7	42,840	45.5	38.9	29.2
Va.	114,046	66.7	37,035	32.4	30.4	25.6
Totals	1,495,513	69.7	566,730	37.9	35.0	27.4

NOTE: The total enrollment for 1927-28 was 33,946 in excess of 1926-27. The pupil capacity of the Rosenwald schools increased 10.5 per cent the past two years.

TABLE VIII—Showing for Comparison Total Number of Rural Negro Schools by States with the Average Number of Pupils Enrolled Per School, the Per Cent the Rosenwald Schools Bear to All Rural Negro Schools and the Number and Average Pupil Capacity of Rosenwald Schools to July 1, 1929.

	Rural Negro Schools				Rosenwald Schools		
	Average No.						
	Pupils en-	Per Cent of all				Average Pupil	
	rolled per	Rural				Capacity	
State	Number	School 7/1/29	7/1/29	7/1/28	No.	7/1/29	7/1/28
Ala.	2,046	68	18.2	17.4	373	97	95
Ark.	1,398	60	21.4	19.5	299	131	125
Fla.	660	75	13.7	9.0	91	194	186
Ga.	2,766	65	7.4	6.5	203	148	143
Ky.	629	46	20.5	18.9	129	98	92
La.	1,337	64	27.8	26.2	372	127	123
Md.	526	55	24.1	22.4	127	93	91
Miss.	3,434	63	14.6	13.8	503	136	136
N. C.........	2,320	81	31.7	29.4	736	138	134
Okla	381	116	40.4	36.2	154	98	97
S. C.	3,182	70	19.6	18.5	429	152	152
Tenn.	1,111	63	29.3	27.3	326	122	118
Texas	1,836	53	21.0	19.2	386	110	108
Va.	1,868	61	17.9	17.2	336	110	109
Totals ..	22,494	65	19.8	18.4	4,464	129	124

"There were 46,193 Negro teachers employed in fourteen Southern States for the year ending June 30, 1928. Of this number 31,843 (68.9 per cent) were in rural schools and 14,350 (31.1 per cent) in the city school systems. The teacher load (number of pupils enrolled per teacher) was 46 in the rural schools and 45 in the city schools. On this score Alabama leads with 60 pupils per teacher, both in rural and city schools, while Kentucky teachers bear the lightest load (36 in rural and 34 in city schools). The number of Negro teachers employed in 1927-28 was 1,029 more than in 1926-27, a gain of 2.2 per cent. This is practically the same as the increase in enrollment for the year 1927-28 (2.3 per cent).

"It is interesting to note the increase in the teacher capacity of the Rosenwald schools in ratio to the total rural teachers employed over each of three years—in 1926-27 only 29.7 per cent, in 1927-28, 35.6 per cent, and in 1928-29, 39.5—even though there has been an increase from year to year in the number of teachers employed. Louisiana leads in the per cent of rural teachers employed which can be accommodated in the Rosenwald schools (56.4 per cent), Arkansas coming

CREEK COUNTY TRAINING SCHOOL, HARLINSVILLE, OKLAHOMA

second (51.0) and North Carolina third (50.6). Georgia continues to hold bottom place (18.1 per cent), while Virginia (28.8) has been forced to second from the bottom by Florida (31.0).

"As the teacher load is decreasing in keeping with the trend in modern education, the number of teachers employed will be relatively greater, which will tend to retard the rate of increase in providing classrooms for all rural Negro teachers employed, as the accompanying table of data by States will show.

TABLE IX—SHOWING TOTAL NUMBER OF NEGRO TEACHERS, THE NUM-
BER, PER CENT AND TEACHER LOAD OF RURAL AND URBAN SEPA-
RATELY, BY STATES.

| | | | Teachers Employed | | | |
| | Total | Rural Teachers | | | Urban Teachers | |
State	Teachers	No.	Per Cent	Load	No.	Per Cent	Load
Ala.	3,015	2,324	77.0	60	691	23.0	60
Ark.	2,391	1,613	67.4	43	778	32.6	56
Fla.	2,148	1,264	58.8	44	884	41.2	42
Ga.	4,937	3,703	75.0	48	1,234	25.0	49
Ky.	1,339	790	59.0	36	549	41.0	34
La.	2,826	1,870	66.1	49	956	33.9	56
Md.	1,319	774	58.6	37	545	41.4	37
Miss.	5,125	4,106	80.1	55	1,019	19.9	47
N. C.	5,959	4,488	75.3	43	1,471	24.7	44
Okla.	1,364	800	58.6	37	564	41.4	35
S. C.	4,451	3,098	69.6	53	1,353	30.4	45
Tenn.	2,800	1,801	64.3	40	999	35.7	43
Tex.	4,722	2,360	49.9	40	2,362	50.1	45
Va.	3,797	2,852	75.1	40	945	24.9	41
Total	46,193	31,843	68.9	47	14,350	31.1	46

"Of the 46,193 Negro teachers employed in fourteen Southern States last year, 21,517 or 46.58 per
cent were enrolled in state approved summer schools
in 1929. This number is somewhat smaller in a few
States than in former years, due to (1) the elimina-
tion of several non-accredited summer schools, (2)
economic conditions, and (3) an increased number of
qualified teachers, particularly in North Carolina.

"While Mississippi had the greatest number of
teachers enrolled in summer schools, Alabama leads
the list in the per cent of teachers in summer schools
(97.74), Mississippi coming second (69.19), and Oklahoma third (54.83). Alabama would still hold first
ranking, even if all the 558 teachers enrolled in Tuskegee Institute were deducted from the total. Table
XI gives this information by States, furnished by
each Department of Education.

TABLE X—SHOWING THE TOTAL RURAL NEGRO TEACHERS EMPLOYED
1927-28, THE TEACHER CAPACITY OF ROSENWALD SCHOOLS, JULY 1,
1929, AND FOR COMPARISON THE PER CENT OF THE TOTAL RURAL
TEACHERS IN ROSENWALD SCHOOLS OVER A THREE YEAR PERIOD.

State	All Rural Schools No. Teachers Employed	Rosenwald Schools Teacher Capacity 7/1/29	Per Cent of all Rural Teachers Employed 7/1/29	7/1/28	7/1/27
Ala.	2,324	810	34.8	29.1	25.9
Ark.	1,613	867	51.0	41.9	30.6
Fla.	1,264	393	31.0	19.7	10.0
Ga.	3,703	670	18.1	15.5	13.4
Ky.	790	283	35.8	30.9	28.7
La.	1,870	1,056	56.4	53.5	48.7
Md.	774	265	34.2	31.3	24.7
Miss.	4,106	1,526	37.1	35.1	28.7
N. C.	4,488	2,270	50.6	46.3	38.3
Okla.	800	338	42.2	37.7	30.9
S. C.	3,098	1,457	47.0	44.9	38.3
Tenn.	1,801	884	49.0	48.9	40.2
Tex.	2,360	952	40.3	37.8	18.9
Va.	2,852	823	28.8	27.3	22.8
Total	31,843	12,594	39.5	35.6	29.7

"Reviewing the statistical report made a year
ago," says Mr. Smith, "it will be seen that the
average term in all the rural Negro schools was 4.7
months in 1914-15 (when Mr. Rosenwald began to
aid in the building of rural Negro schools), 6.0 months
in 1925-26, and 6.5 months in 1926-27.

"It is interesting to see that the average term of
the Rosenwald schools on which building aid was
given in 1925-26 was about three-fourths of a month
longer than that of all rural Negro schools, and in
1926-27 one-half month longer. The average term of
the Rosenwald schools built by years from 1925-26
to 1928-29, increased gradually each year as follows:
1925-26, 6.7 months; 1926-27, 7.0 months; 1927-28, 7.2
months, and 1928-29, 7.4 months. This clearly indi-

TABLE XI—TOTAL TEACHERS EMPLOYED (1927-28) AND PER CENT
ENROLLED IN STATE APPROVED SUMMER SCHOOLS (1929)

Teachers

State	Total No. Employed	No. Attending Summer School	Per Cent in S. S.	No. of Approved Summer Schools
Ala.	3.015	2,947 [1]	97.74	6
Ark.	2,391	953	35.67	4
Fla.	2,148	695	32.35	3
Ga.	4,937	1,884	38.16	4
Ky.	1,339	600	44.80	3
La.	2,826	1,348	47.70	9
Md.	1,319	154 [3]	11.67 [3]	2
Miss.	5,125	3,546	69.19	19
N. C.	5,939	2,150	36.07	9
Okla.	1,364	748	54.83	2
S. C.	4,451	1,844	41.42	3
Tenn.	2,800	1,213	43.32	2
Tex.	4,722	1,677	35.14	4
Va.	3,797	1,178 [2]	46.30	6
Totals	46,193	21,517	46.58	76
West Virginia		142		1
		21,659		77

TABLE XII—AVERAGE LENGTH OF TERM IN ALL RURAL NEGRO SCHOOLS
1914-15, 1925-26, AND 1926-27, AND FOR ROSENWALD SCHOOLS
BUILT 1925-26, 1926-27, 1927-28, AND 1928-29.

Average Length of Rural School Term in Months

	All Rural Negro Schools			Rosenwald Schools Built			
State	1914-15	1925-26	1926-27	1925-26	1926-27	1927-28	1928-29
Ala.	4.4	4.7	6.1	6.6	6.1	6.5	7.1
Ark.	4.8	6.0	6.3	7.0	7.1	7.1	7.3
Fla.	4.0	5.0	5.1	6.6	6.6	6.6	7.0
Ga.	5.0	6.0	6.0	7.9	7.0	7.5	7.9
Ky.	6.0	7.0	7.5	7.4	7.7	7.5	8.1
La.	3.0	5.0	4.5	6.3	6.8	6.5	7.1
Md.	7.0	8.7	8.3	8.3	8.3	8.0	8.5
Miss.	3.5	5.3	6.0	7.0	7.1	7.4	7.1
N. C.	5.0	6.4	5.3	6.3	6.7	6.8	6.8
Okla.	6.7	7.0	8.0	7.4	7.9	8.1	8.1
S. C.	3.2	4.8	4.8	5.9	5.9	6.9	6.6
Tenn.	4.5	7.0	7.0	7.4	8.0	8.2	8.3
Tex.	4.5	5.0	5.8	7.0	7.1	7.2	7.6
Va.	5.0	6.8	6.9	6.8	7.0	7.5	7.5
Total ..	4.7	6.0	6.5	6.7	7.0	7.2	7.4

cates that the average term in the Rosenwald schools is longer than in the average rural Negro school by approximately one month. Data by States are shown in table XII.

TABLE XIII—SHOWING BY STATES TOTAL COUNTIES, NUMBER HAVING ROSENWALD SCHOOLS, NUMBER NEW COUNTIES BUILDING SCHOOLS 1928-29, AND NUMBER WITH 5 PER CENT OR MORE NEGRO POPULATION HAVING NO ROSENWALD SCHOOLS.

STATE	Total Number Counties	No. Having Rosenwald Schools	New Counties Building Schools the Past Year	No. With 5 Per Cent or More Negro Population Having No Rosenwald Schools
Ala.	67	63	2	2
Ark.	75	44	2	5
Fla.	67	32	6	29
Ga.	161	93	7	54
Ky.	120	54	2	22
La.	64	58	2	6
Md.	23	20	0	0
Miss.	82	75	2	8
N. C.	100	89	3	3
Okla.	77	39	3	1
S. C.	46	46	0	0
Tenn.	95	59	7	9
Tex.	253	73	3	26
Va.	100	73	1	14
Totals	1,330	818	40	179

"Three years ago the Julius Rosenwald Fund offered aid in stimulating high school development by raising the maximum type of schools on which aid would be given from a six-teacher to a nine-teacher, which was raised to a ten-teacher type or larger, beginning July 1, 1927. This extra aid toward the construction of larger buildings, furnishing additional rooms for high school pupils, has produced most satisfactory results in all the Southern States, as may be seen by referring to Table XIV which shows by States the distribution of the 260 two- to four-year high schools built.

TABLE XIV—SCHOOLS WITH HIGH SCHOOL GRADES OF FROM 2 TO 4
    YEARS ON WHICH THE FUND GAVE AID 1926-27, 1927-28 AND
    1928-29.

		1928-29		Totals for 3 Years		
State	Total	2-3 Yr.	4 Yr.	Total	2-3 Yr.	4 Yr.
Ala.	3	2	1	9	8	1
Ark.	5	4	1	12	6	6
Fla.	6	1	5	12	5	7
Ga.	8	6	2	26	23	3
Ky.	5	1	4	5	1	4
La.	9	3	6	15	6	9
Md.	3	0	3	5	1	4
Miss.	5	4	1	15	11	4
N. C.	18	4	14	49	17	32
Okla.	1	0	1	16	10	6
S. C.	7	7	0	20	17	3
Tenn.	8	5	3	24	17	7
Tex.	14	12	2	43	39	4
Va.	2	2	0	9	9	0
Totals	94	51	43	260	170	90

"In this three year period (July 1, 1926, to July 1, 1929), 90 four-year high schools were built by aid of the Fund—29 in 1926-27, 18 in 1927-28, and 43 in 1928-29. North Carolina led in this group with more than one-third the total (32), Louisiana coming second (9), and Florida and Tennessee tying for third place (7 each). No doubt some of the two- to three-year schools have grown into the four-year group since the last reports were received.

"There were 170 two- to three-year high schools built by aid of the Fund in this three-year period, with Texas leading (39), Georgia coming second (23), and North Carolina, South Carolina, and Tennessee tying for third place (17 each).

"For the past year the Fund has further encouraged high school service by giving aid to extend terms, enabling several schools to qualify for high school accreditment on this score by increasing the term to nine months, and helping a larger number of rural schools to increase their terms to eight months qualifying for aid under the Slater Fund as County Training. All of these schools do at least two years of high school work and many have three to four years.

"Transportation aid was given as an experiment in three counties in Alabama in 1928-29, to transport rural pupils to central county training schools, and

POTTAWATTOMIE COUNTY TRAINING SCHOOL, BROOKSVILLE, OKLAHHOMA

extended to other Southern States, beginning July, 1929, with a hope of stimulating the development of consolidation and high school facilities.

"Stimulated by this new phase of the work, several States are planning to furnish complete high school facilities to a number of counties in 1929-30 by use of transportation buses. This promises to be the most effective means of giving to the rural Negro pupils high school opportunities—about the only way to furnish high school services to a majority of these pupils.

"The rural library has not only helped the elementary pupils but has enabled many county training and high schools to qualify for accreditment. The high school library on which aid will be given by the Julius Rosenwald Fund for the first time in 1929-30 will greatly increase the number of standard high

THE SCHOOL IN THE COMMUNITY SUITE

schools, and at the same time increase the efficiency of these schools as well as the interest and pleasure of the pupils.

"Mr. Lee M. Favrot has made a most careful and comprehensive study of Negro high schools which was published in the *High School Quarterly,* April, 1929, making it unnecessary to comment further on high schools. It is encouraging to see that the enrollment in all Negro high schools of fourteen Southern States 1927-28 was 75,631 pupils (9.8 for every 1,000 population), the number of high school teachers, 3,572, and four-year high school graduates, 8,958.

"The 4,464 Rosenwald schools completed to July, 1929, were 19.8 per cent of all rural Negro schools (22,494) in these States, according to the latest available reports for all schools. Oklahoma ranks highest in the per cent the Rosenwald schools bear to all rural Negro schools (40.0), North Carolina second (31.7), and Tennessee third (29.3), while Georgia occupies

ROSENWALD SCHOOL AT DAYTON, TENNESSEE

bottom place (7.4), Florida holding momentarily second place (13.7), and Mississippi third place from the bottom (14.6). But Florida made the greatest gain in the per cent the past year (4.7) with Oklahoma running a close second (4.2).

"The average size of all rural Negro schools measured by pupils enrolled is 65 (1.42 teachers) while that of the Rosenwald schools is 129 (2.82 teachers), or practically double the size of the average rural Negro schools.

"Some counties have not yet been touched by this rural school construction. Of these 179 counties in these fourteen Southern States with 5 per cent or more Negro population having no Rosenwald schools," says Mr. Smith, "24 counties have more than 50 per cent each—Georgia leading with 21, Louisiana, Mississippi and Virginia 1 each. Georgia has 12 such counties with more than 60 per cent Negro population and 5 with 70 per cent, and Virginia has 1 with more than 60 per cent. There are 19 counties with a Negro population of between 40 and 50 per cent that have no Rosenwald schools, Georgia leading with 8, Florida 7, Alabama, Louisiana, Mississippi and North Carolina 1 each. There are still 68 counties each having a relative Negro population equal to or greater than the average in the South (28.0 per cent), which built no Rosenwald school, to July 1, 1929. These 279 counties have 218,730 scholastics (a number equal to the total rural Negro children of school age in Florida, Kentucky, Maryland and Oklahoma) and a total enrollment of 163,384 pupils.

"But stimulated largely by the extra aid for backward counties in 1928-29—one and one-half times the regular allotment for the first Rosenwald school built in a county—40 new counties were added to the list the past year. The 4,464 Rosenwald schools built to July 1, 1929, are located in 818 counties of the fourteen States. South Carolina has two or more Rosenwald schools in every one of the 46 counties, and Maryland, in all but two counties, and these have practically no Negro population."

What the prospects are no one can tell. The Julius Rosenwald Fund offers no such promise as a perpetual building program. This policy would seem to

TABLE XV—SUMMARY OF COUNTIES IN FOURTEEN SOUTHERN STATES HAVING 5 PER CENT OR MORE NEGRO POPULATION AND NO ROSENWALD SCHOOLS, SHOWING SCHOLASTICS AND ENROLLMENT BY STATES.

State	No. Counties	Scholastics	Enrollment
Ala.	2	13,224	10,606
Ark.	5	4,837	3,257
Fla	29	50,106	29,120
Ga.	54	67,905	50,797
Ky.	22	6,609	5,562
La.	6	11,679	4,446
Md.	0	.....	.....
Miss.	8	13,816	9,348
N. C.	3	No report	3,517
Okla.	1	3,894	No report
S. C.	0	.....	.....
Tenn.	9	1,619	1,521
Tex.	26	45,031	36,512
Va.	14	No report	8,698
Totals	179	218,720	163,384

indicate that it has endeavored to stimulate self-help rather than to encourage dependency of the Negroes and their friends on assistance from without. Inasmuch as the contributions from the people and the appropriations of the state for Negro education now exceed the moneys appropriated to this purpose by the Fund it is highly probable that at some time in the near future appropriations from this source will not be necessary. If such a thing can be achieved, the Fund will have wisely served the cause of social uplift in a much more efficient way than any help which Negro education has so far received.

There are in the South, moreover, certain changes of attitude which indicate that the Fund has been instrumental in effecting a revolution in Southern sentiment which will make it possible to withdraw from this field. Certain State departments of public instruction, a number of county authorities, and some of the local school boards of the South have reached the conclusion that there should be no discrimination in the apportionment of school funds. Although the races are to be educated in separate schools, each one must have a chance to develop. In a few places in the South, therefore, the Negro building program is receiving its pro rata share of funds appropriated for this purpose, and the teachers are being paid practically the same salaries. In this case, of course, there is just a beginning. It will require much time

AN AGRICULTURAL DISTRICT IMPROVED BY A SCHOOL

yet before these inequalities can be worked out. For some years, the policy of equal school facilities has been followed in the cities of St. Louis, Baltimore, and Washington, and it is gradually finding its way into the smaller cities and towns of the upper South.

More extensive, however, is the policy of permitting the expansion of the curriculum in the Negro schools. Having learned that practical education advocated by Booker T. Washington is after all useful for both races, the whites have less tendency to restrict the

Negroes altogether to training of this sort. Realizing, too, that there can be no progress in education without an efficient teaching corps, Southern school officials are willing to do more for the advanced training of Negroes and especially for teachers. The County Training Schools, promoted by the John F. Slater Fund with the aid of the General Education Board, have actually become high schools, although they do not bear that name. In sections where these schools

AN OLD BUILDING YIELDS GROUND TO THE NEW

have not been provided, Negro high schools are being established and they are being designated as high schools. In these institutions they generally offer the same course of study as that found in those for the whites. There is also a tendency to provide better equipment and to employ teachers, who in contradistinction to those who heretofore have been appointed by personal favor, must have actual qualifications for doing the work according to modern standards.

In the State schools, in which has been provided the highest education offered the Negroes at public expense, there has also been a tendency upward. These schools, formerly restricted to education in the fundamentals, in trades and vocations, have been permitted to expand such curricula into those of well equipped technical schools and teachers' colleges. It has been clearly demonstrated that only persons of developed minds can work efficiently and to provide for such mental equipment, there must be a professionally trained body of teachers. Going still further in this direction, some of these State schools offer also a liberal arts course for those Negroes who may be interested in things purely cultural or who may aspire to the study of law and medicine.

To encourage these State departments of education in this direction, unusual impetus has been given to other efforts by the aid received from the General Education Board. Tending to restrict themselves to assisting those schools best circumstanced to render the greatest service to the largest number, the General Education Board has recently appropriated considerable sums of money to a few State institutions. The aim is to assist in carrying out the building program in the effort to maintain for the Negroes in each State at least one institution where they may obtain the highest training provided for others. In States like Florida, Tennessee, and North Carolina, therefore, the program of education has made such headway as to show bright prospects for a new day. The Julius Rosenwald movement, laying the foundation for the super-structure upon which these new forces have had to build, has made a larger contribution than we can at this time appreciate.

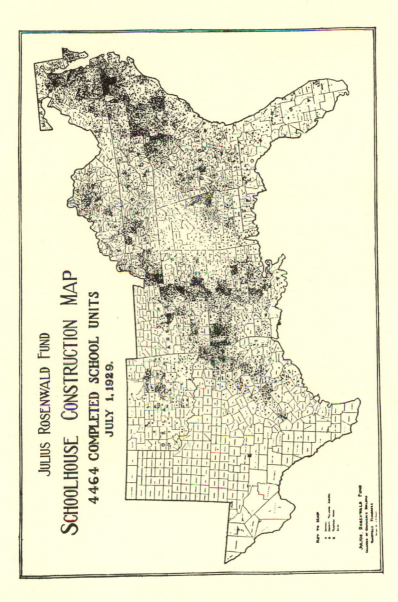

JULIUS ROSENWALD FUND

SCHOOLHOUSE CONSTRUCTION MAP

4464 COMPLETED SCHOOL UNITS

JULY 1, 1929.

CHAPTER XII

DISCOURAGING ASPECT OF THINGS

ENCOURAGING as these recent developments may be, however, the Negro peasant has not yet much of a chance to be what is commonly known as a free man. In the East, North, and West, where the Negroes are not found in rural communities in large numbers racial restrictions are not so rigid or do not apparently exist. In the cities of these sections such customary restrictions are softened by what the Negroes in large numbers are influential enough to do for themselves. In the other parts, in the South and especially in the lower rural South, social repression of the Negro is the rule of life. The whites are insane enough to believe that they are inherently superior to the blacks, that the whites have achieved everything worth while, that they are divinely ordained, as a better class which must maintain its "integrity" in order to preserve the "wonderful civilization" earmarked by their "Almighty" as "Anglo-Saxon," "Caucasian," or "Christian." This being the case, it is necessary to set up between the whites and blacks numerous insurmountable barriers to prevent the intermarriage of the races.

In other words, they confess that although the white man is "superior" to the Negro, there is something about the Negro sufficiently attractive to lead the white to seek intermarriage. White persons,

then, must be restrained by the will of the majority of their group. While there may be a few
not in full accord with this program, they dare not
diverge therefrom, for it is the community speaking
with superior force to the individual who must sacrifice his own interests in behalf of the ''divinely ordained integrity of the white race and its perpetua-
tion as the leader of modern culture.''

To prevent miscegenation the program is very well
defined and in most cases rigidly carried out. Whites
and Negroes must have nothing to do with each other
except when the latter is serving the former in menial
capacity or in business transactions, and even then
white women must have no dealings with Negro men.
If white men take unto themselves Negro concubines,
that is not so deplorable, although not desirable here
and there. Enforced segregation in housing, transportation, education, and places of amusement is a
necessity, then, in the carrying out of this program
of life. Negroes and whites must select their friends
from their own respective races. While Negroes under the possible penalty of loss of life must be cour-
teous and submissive to whites at all times, white
people must not extend to them similar courtesies.
Far from being a mere custom or a principle of government, it has become a religion, against which the
teachings of the liberal element avail nothing.

The priesthood of this religious caste emphasize
the belief in the traditional God of the Hebrews but
preach against the principles of justice which He
revealed. They profess Jesus of Nazareth but militantly array themselves against living according to
the brotherhood which He taught. In fact, they will
wade through blood to prevent any such humanity of

man to man.   They have done so, and will do it again to
prevent any radical change.   When they fail to find
some passage of scripture which can be illogically
construed to support their position, they fall back
on the divinely ordained leadership of the Caucasians,
which has been such a blessing to the world in the
extension of their dominion over weaker and helpless
peoples.   In other words, they recite the story and
present numerous instances of how their god has

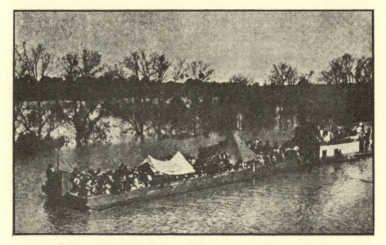

CARRYING NEGRO PEONS BACK TO THE PLANTATIONS

intervened in their behalf and brought them safe thus
far.   If they continue as they have heretofore, then,
this god will bring them still greater conquests.   From
their racial point of view, white men do not need to
worry about enslaving blacks, reducing the free Negroes to peonage, disfranchising them, and prevent-
ing them from being enlightened or from rising in the
economic sphere.   Their god has always sanctioned
these things in the interest of race distinction by
divine right.   In no case has their god taught social

equality. It is divinely ordained, they believe, that a large portion of the human family must be kept in drudgery to serve the fortunate few who seriously apply themselves to literature, philosophy, and politics. Praise, therefore, be to this blessed god! Let white people rejoice! Let Negroes be afraid and keep in their place to which this god has assigned them; and if they do not, their punishment or extermination is justifiable in the sight of this god.

To keep in their place, Negroes must address all white persons with the title of "Mister," "Madam," "Miss," etc., and take off their hats in greeting whites, although no white man must treat the Negroes likewise. In answering whites Negroes must say, "No Sir," "No Madam," "No Miss," etc., instead of merely "No." Negroes must not expect white persons to shake their hands and should not embarrass themselves by extending them. When Negroes have any business to transact with white persons at their homes they must go around to the back door, and if they happen to go into the innermost part of the house, they must not take seats, for the chairs would have to be renovated, destroyed, or burned.

In 1927, B. E. Mays, a very well educated and intelligent social welfare worker then serving as Secretary of the Tampa Urban League, took the popular band of the Negro State College of Florida to the home of a rich man in Tampa to give a concert. After presenting them and starting them off with the first number Mays took a seat, thinking that the lady of the house had nodded such assent; but she hurried across the room to him and made him get up. A Negro mulatto once visited a Southern white woman in the interest of his school. Thinking that he was white, she courteously asked him to take a seat. Upon finding out later that he had Negro blood in his veins, she destroyed the chair in which he sat.

In all things Negroes must await their turn. If a Negro works in the home of a white person he must wait until the members of the family have been served their meals and then he may have his in the kitchen, on the back porch, or in the back yard. While

DESTROYED BY THE FLOOD

the whites feast on the best, moreover, the Negroes must be content with the coarsest food or the scraps from the whites' table. In places like stores, where there may be crowds, Negroes must not insist on being waited on in their turn. If the clerks choose to wait on all the whites first and then direct their attention to the Negroes they can neither say nor do anything about it. For business reasons this rule cannot always be enforced where there is keen competition, but at the post office inquiring for mail, or in the station purchasing tickets, Negroes must observe this rule; for it generally obtains without an appreciable variation.

There is no statutory law to enforce these things, but custom here is stronger than law; or here is a revival of the personality of law once existent among the barbarians of Germany. Law for the Negro in these backward parts is the will of the white man with whom the Negro may happen to deal. If there is no positive measure which a white man may invoke in enforcing his will against the Negro all he needs to do is to appeal to the mob, raise the hue and cry, and the Negro pays the penalty.

Apparently, however, there is just as much security for the Negroes in these parts as in any other section of the country. The Negroes get along well with the whites until one of the latter claims that some Negro has offended him. Unless the white man is one of the poorest of the poor complaining against a Negro who is under the protection of some prominent white, the Negro is helpless in the situation. No white man as a rule will believe a Negro in preference to one of his own race. The Negro, therefore, cannot actually testify against a white person in the rural courts, and the jury, the bench, and the bar are constituted by white persons who represent an antagonistic class. The formal testimony of Negroes against whites may be heard and other formalities may be observed, but judgment has already preceded proof.

Knowing that such is the attitude of these local courts, Negroes in the rural districts are reduced to the necessity of going into the service or seeking the protection of influential white persons. In the case of a clash with some white person invoking the law will avail nothing, but it will help the Negro tremendously to have some white planter or business man to say "He is a good nigger. He is in my employ. He is all right. Let him go." And thus it is often done. In this way many a poor Negro has been saved from imprisonment or death. A Negro proceeding independently has no recourse but flight. In the case of a Negro in a town charged with an

PREPARING FOR SLAUGHTER

offense not penalized by law the vigilantes assembled and served notice on him to leave town on the next train. He thanked them for their consideration and informed them that he could do better than that. He would catch the train that had just left.

Exactly how this attachment to influential whites has worked in the case of the Negroes' economic and other rights, however, will be better appreciated by observing the influence of this custom on the development of peonage. Here we see the same tendency that appeared in the breakup of the Roman Empire when the invading hordes made it necessary for the weak and poor to "commend" themselves to the protection of the influential owners of large landed estates. Out of this came feudalism. Out of peonage we have something like a continuation of slavery.

Nothing illustrates this survival of the personality of law better than the treatment of Negroes in traffic cases which have been multiplied by the good roads and the rise of the automobile. An agent of the National Benefit Life Insurance Company working in North Carolina reported to the head office in Washington in 1929 that an insurance man in that State refused to sell him any insurance on his automobile for the reason that, should he have a collision with a white man's machine, the courts would force the Negro to pay the damages, even if it could be shown that the white man was at fault. An investigator of the Association for the Study of Negro Life and History while studying conditions in Georgia had the running board of his car smashed by a white woman just as he was turning into the main street of Macon. He got out of his car and took the number of the colliding machine. The white lady, being a woman of culture, acknowledged it as her fault, and gave him her father's address that he might call upon him to have the car repaired. In the meantime a mob of white hoodlums gathered around him saying: "What are you doing talking to that white woman, nigger? Get into that car and get away from here." The investigator kept cool, doing at the same time all he could to straighten out the running board which in its broken condition prevented one wheel from turning. Finally he adjusted matters and moved away from the gathering mob before they did him bodily injury. When he went to present the case to the young lady's father in his office the next day at nine o'clock, the old man drove him out into the vestibule and cursed him, calling him all the things which Negroes are under the circumstances, and he was lucky to get away with only that.

A little semblance of fairness, however, may be found here and there. An agent of the Associated Publishers working in Cary, Mississippi, reported in August, 1929, "On Saturday, July 13, I had an unavoidable collision with a white lady, in which neither she nor any of my passengers, or I were hurt, but both cars were damaged; mine more. Had she not exprest that it was as much her fault as mine I would've been lodged in jail. She had just past me going in the same direction. She aimed to make a fly turn across the highway and found her turn-road blocked with plantation mules. Hence, she had to make a sudden stop. I was too close to stop without hitting the rear of her car, so I pulled to the left to go around and just as my car reached the rear of hers she pulled across the highway, thus causing me to strike the running board of her car. The running board was the only visible damage sustained by her car. Yet, her father enumerates damages to several hundred dollars and wants me to pay same. I had an interview with him but couldn't get him to reason with me at all; so I wrote him a nice letter after returning home and I feel he'll reconsider the matter. The sheriff was soon on the scene after the collision, but after investigating didn't attempt to arrest me. Instead, he told me, that from the evidence obtained from eye-witnesses, he was of the opinion the girl's father would tell me to fix my car and he (the father) would fix his. I hope such will be the outcome. Altho, I'm in Dixie.''

In large urban centers of the South one finds a few liberal-minded whites who have been cured of the race insanity which afflicts the Negroes with so many ills, but in the rural districts it is about as rampant as ever. There has recently been a decrease in the lynching of Negroes because guardians of the law

THE MOB IN ACTION

have at last come to recognize that terrorism of the laboring class is not a good thing for the economic development of the country and, therefore, have ceased to abet such lawlessness. The rank and file of the people in the backwoods, however, have not changed their attitude, and if the Negroes disregarded these unwritten laws of repression there would be more violence than ever. Peace in so many of these communities means that the Negroes have acquiesced into occupying an inferior position in the

social order.   Unfortunately, too, interracial coöperation about which we hear so much signifies mainly
the keeping of the Negroes satisfied with getting less
than their share of the loaf, while the whites are being
persuaded to be a little more lenient.   These interracial coworkers dare not attack the general policy
of race distinction and segregation.   If they did they
could not operate in the South.   They have accom-

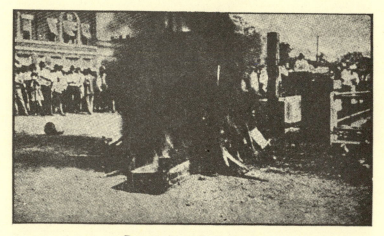

BURNING THE BODY ALIVE

plished much good in spots, but the results of their
efforts are easily overestimated.

For the present, then, the rural Negroes, and most
urban Negroes so far as that is concerned, must be
denied equal facilities of education, "driven out of
the Church of Christ, excluded from inns, labeled like
chattel in traveling, refused decent employment,
forced to pay the highest rent for the poorest homes;
prohibited from buying property in decent neighbor-
hoods, ridiculed in the press, on the platform, and
on the stage; disfranchised, taxed without represen-

tation; denied the right to choose their friends or to be chosen by them; deprived by custom and law of protection for their women, robbed of justice in the courts and lynched with impunity."[1]

And what can the Negro do about it? Nothing. If he is to live in these parts he must accept these conditions and keep his mouth shut. If he does not

CIVILIZATION IN THE BACKWOODS

like the place assigned to him here he may go to Africa where he will fare worse. The Bourbon press, then, can all but truthfully say: "Our Negroes down here are quiet. You never hear a word of complaint unless it comes from the professional agitators up North. Let us, therefore, run things down here. We understand the Negroes and they understand us." Most assuredly they do.

[1] *The Crisis*, June, 1924.

Sometimes one inquires as to what the enlightened Negroes are doing to direct attention to these things. The inevitable answer is that they are doing absolutely nothing in the open. What bearing their service has on the situation is indirect. The intelligent Negroes in the South are more timid than the riffraff. The Southern whites stand less in fear of the schooled Negroes than they do of the rabble. When cornered the Negro rough element will sometimes fight it out down to death, but under such circumstances the Christianized Negroes hold indignation meetings or take their troubles to God in prayer. Furthermore, Negroes who are outspoken are not allowed to remain in these neglected districts, and those who are appointed to teach or who are allowed to preach and conduct business must demonstrate in some way that they willingly accept the status assigned and will encourage their fellows to remain in a state of harmless equipoise. There must be no neutral ground, moreover; a man is either for the régime or against it. If he is not willing to declare himself in favor of it, he cannot expect any unusual favors from the whites, and he becomes an object of suspicion. In case of any inexplicable trouble, too, circumstantial evidence will point to those not supposedly obsequious in their dealings with the whites.

Reading the constitutions and laws of the South, which apparently put a premium on education and the ownership of property, an uninformed person might inquire as to why the Negroes do not qualify more generally as voters and thus compel the authorities to grant them more consideration. These laws, however, although not thus worded, are intended to eliminate the Negro voters as factors in the body politic. Registration clerks refuse to register Negroes in most places, giving some evasive explanation or driving them out of the office. Very few of these election officials go to the trouble of a subterfuge examination to make such points as inability to explain certain parts of the constitution, the failure to pay a certain tax, or to register at a certain time. In some cases of actual registration by Negroes the

THE BREAD-LINE AFTER THE FLOOD

officials contrive to lose by election day the book in which they are registered.

To show how generally this is applied one needs but remember that only a few years ago a swarthy, well educated white teacher of a Southern school, being taken for a Negro, was denied the right to vote there because he could not explain certain parts of the constitution, although he is a graduate of an accredited Northern university. Where the operation of these laws did not succeed in eliminating the Negro voters bulldozing, terrorism, and slaughter were resorted to until the Negroes of these parts acquiesced in the abandonment of all political rights. In North Carolina, for example, where so much is now being done to enlighten the Negroes, one could hardly interest any group of them in the local political matters of any district or county. Mrs. Owen, the head of the Alabama Department of Archives and History, expressed her interest in seeing intelligent, property-owning Negroes vote. She was surprised to learn on investigation that in 1926 only 1,500 Negroes actually voted in Alabama; but another observer reported 3,500 Negro voters in Alabama in 1928.[1] Asking the Negro educator at the head of the State Normal School whether or not he voted, Mrs. Owen was informed by him that the commissioners required of him a thing which even a Negro of this type cannot easily do. He was told that he would have to get three influential white persons to recommend him for this privilege, and he found the terms too difficult to press the matter further.[2]

According to Dr. DuBois, who has given attention to these matters, especially in 1928, about five and a half million Negroes are of voting age. A million and a half of these are illiterate. About four million should vote, according to laws of this country and of the States. In Virginia, North Carolina, Oklahoma, and Texas, a number of Negroes exercise the right of suffrage in national elections, but are ineffective at other times. Almost three million of these Negroes are actually disfranchised by the operation of the laws in South Carolina, Georgia, Florida, Alabama, Mississippi, and Louisiana. In the presidential election of 1928 only 980 Negroes were registered voters

[1] *The Crisis*, June, 1928.
[2] Mrs. Owen made this statement to the author.

in Louisiana; and 3,500 in Alabama, 22 being at Tuskegee, 41 at Montgomery, 958 at Mobile, and less than 1,000 at Birmingham. In Mississippi, 3,454 registered, according to one official, whereas another believed that it was a little less than 2,000. Fifteen Negroes are allowed to vote in Baton Rouge.[1]

In a few Negro settlements the situation is different. Negroes actually control the local governments in such places. Sometimes they have influence in white or mixed settlements nearby. C. J. Calloway, of Tuskegee, in presenting the author to the County Superintendent of Macon County, Alabama, inquired about the results of the bond issue election and informed the undersigned that he voted at that precinct and was active in its civic affairs.

[1] *The Crisis*, November, 1928.

APPENDIX

TABLE XVI. — NEGRO CHURCHES — VALUE OF CHURCH EDIFICES AND DEBT

[Urban territory includes all cities and other incorporated places which had 2,500 inhabitants or more

	DENOMINATION	Number of church edifices	ALL CHURCHES				
			Value of church edifices			Debt on church edifices	
			Churches reporting	Amount (dollars)	Average per church (dollars)	Churches reporting	Amount (dollars)
1	**All denominations**...............	37,749	37,347	205,782,628	5,510	8,884	22,178,581
	Adventist bodies:						
2	Advent Christian Church.............	5	3	4,950	1,650	....	....
3	Seventh-day Adventist Denomination....	81	78	789,400	10,121	33	155,215
4	African Orthodox Church	2	2	30,000	15,000	2	9,000
5	African Orthodox Church of New York......	1	1	50,000	....	1	12,100
6	Apostolic Overcoming Holy Church of God..	10	10	16,950	1,695	5	1,975
	Baptist bodies:						
7	Negro Baptists......................	20,011	19,833	103,465,759	5,217	3,743	10,533,174
8	United American Free Will Baptist Church...........................	144	142	308,425	2,172	39	7,962
9	Colored Primitive Baptists............	91	87	171,518	1,971	15	9,793
10	Christian and Missionary Alliance........	6	6	57,625	9,604	3	23,050
11	Christian Church (General Convention of the Christian Church).................	56	56	235,100	5,091	15	15,401
12	Church of Christ, Holiness.	69	68	326,850	4,807	20	79,224
13	Church of Christ, Scientist..............	1	1	254,061	....	1	233,561
14	Church of God.....................	15	15	78,015	5,201	10	19,737
15	Church of God (headquarters,Anderson,Ind.)	81	77	343,450	4,460	29	66,367
16	Church of God and Saints of Christ........	49	48	149,210	3,109	20	30,219
17	Church of God in Christ..................	531	516	1,508,079	2,923	234	261,611
18	Church of Christ.......................	141	141	139,919	992	21	4,816
19	Churches of God, Holiness...............	16	16	159,700	9,981	7	71,375
20	Churches of God in North America (General Eldership)...........................	5	3	8,000	2,667	....	....
	Churches of the Living God:						
21	Church of the Living God, Christian Workers for Fellowship	141	139	368,935	2,654	27	26,460
22	Church of the Living God, "The Pillar and Ground of Truth"...............	84	81	170,547	2,106	45	29,277
23	Congregational Churches................	145	139	1,896,415	13,643	59	230,470
24	Disciples of Christ.....................	421	411	1,495,568	3,639	94	210,410
25	Free Christian Zion Church of Christ.......	4	4	22,000	5,500	1	275
26	Free Church of God in Christ.............	11	11	23,700	2,155	8	7,200
27	Independent etc., churches..............	2	2	67,000	33,500	2	30,100
	Lutheran bodies:						
28	United Lutheran Church in America.....	1	1	13,000	....	....	....
29	Evangelical Lutheran Synodical Conference of America— Evangelical Lutheran Synod of Missouri, Ohio, and Other States........	57	55	339,650	6,175	5	13,790
	Methodist bodies:						
30	Methodist Episcopal Church	3,572	3,552	18,938,246	5,332	1,095	2,389,675
31	Methodist Protestant Church...........	44	44	91,650	2,083	9	4,998

in 1920, the date of the last Federal census; rural territory comprises the remainder of the country]

	URBAN CHURCHES						RURAL CHURCHES					
		Value of church edifices			Debt on church edifices			Value of church edifices			Debt on church edifices	
Number of church edifices	Churches reporting	Amount (dollars)	Average per church (dollars)	Churches reporting	Amount (dollars)	Number of church edifices	Churches reporting	Amount (dollars)	Average per church (dollars)	Churches reporting	Amount (dollars)	
9,124	8,952	145,730,958	16,279	3,961	19,642,007	28,625	28,395	60,051,670	2,115	4,923	2,536,574	1
1	1	4,000	......	.....	....	4	2	950	475	.....	....	2
77	74	785,100	10,609	33	155,215	4	4	4,300	1,075	.....	....	3
2	2	30,000	15,000	2	9,000	......	......	....	....	.....	....	4
1	1	50,000	......	1	12,000	......	......	....	....	.....	....	5
6	6	12,100	2,017	2	1,600	4	4	4,850	1,213	3	375	6
4,072	4,012	69,444,724	17,309	1,726	9,385,537	15,939	15,821	34,021,035	2,150	2,017	1,147,637	7
9	9	53,900	5,989	3	1,243	135	133	254,525	1,914	36	6,719	8
27	26	93,870	3,610	8	7,259	64	61	77,648	1,273	7	2,534	9
5	5	55,625	11,125	3	23,050	1	1	2,000	......	.....	....	10
8	8	168,000	21,000	3	11,000	48	48	117,100	2,440	12	4,401	11
37	36	274,750	7,632	13	76,153	32	32	52,100	1,628	7	3,071	12
1	1	245,061	......	1	233,561	......	......	....	....	.....	....	13
5	5	57,000	11,400	2	15,240	10	10	21,015	2,102	8	4,497	14
48	45	305,150	6,781	21	64,702	33	32	38,300	1,197	8	1,665	15
43	42	138,860	3,306	19	30,130	6	6	10,350	1,725	1	89	16
300	288	1,274,353	4,425	160	242,061	231	228	233,726	1,025	74	19,550	17
49	49	90,010	1,837	7	3,301	92	92	49,909	542	14	1,515	18
11	11	152,500	13,864	6	71,350	5	5	7,200	1,440	1	25	19
3	1	6,200	......	.....	....	2	2	1,800	900	.....	....	20
77	75	268,750	3,583	21	24,240	64	64	100,185	1,565	6	2,220	21
48	45	126,665	2,815	30	24,960	36	36	43,882	1,219	15	4,317	22
90	85	1,733,700	20,396	38	224,025	55	54	162,715	3,013	21	6,445	23
147	140	1,058,900	7,564	57	196,119	274	271	436,668	1,611	37	14,291	24
1	1	16,000	......	1	275	3	3	6,000	2,000	.....	....	25
10	10	23,200	2,320	7	7,000	1	1	500	......	1	200	26
2	2	67,000	33,500	2	30,100	......	......	....	....	.....	....	27
1	1	13,000	......	.....	....	......	......	....	....	.....	....	28
25	23	293,500	12,761	4	13,640	32	32	46,150	1,442	1	150	29
769	758	12,914,353	17,037	369	2,048,398	2,803	2,794	6,023,893	2,156	726	341,277	30
9	9	26,000	2,889	3	3,155	35	35	65,650	1,876	6	1,843	31

243

	DENOMINATION	Number of church edifices	ALL CHURCHES				
			Value of church edifices			Debt on church edifices	
			Churches reporting	Amount (dollars)	Average per church (dollars)	Churches reporting	Amount (dollars)
32	Wesleyan Methodist Connection (or Church) of America...............	22	22	83,100	3,777	1	3,600
33	African Methodist Episcopal Church.......	5,927	5,829	32,092,549	5,506	1,908	3,332,972
34	African Methodist Episcopal Zion Church.	2,370	2,370	18,515,723	7,813	514	1,837,352
35	Colored Methodist Protestant Church....	3	3	36,000	12,000	1	1,200
36	Union American Methodist Episcopal Church.......................	65	64	478,951	7,484	23	42,294
37	African Union Methodist Protestant Church	43	40	476,269	11,907	17	21,925
38	Colored Methodist Episcopal Church.....	2,346	2,341	9,211,437	3,935	591	960,124
39	Reformed Zion Union Apostolic Church...	46	45	184,075	4,091	17	11,681
40	Reformed Methodist Union Episcopal Church.......................	28	21	74,800	3,562	5	3,710
41	Independent African Methodist Episcopal Church.......................	29	28	98,050	3,502	14	35,619
	Moravian bodies:						
42	Moravian Church in America..........	1	1	30,000	....	....	....
	Presbyterian bodies:						
43	Presbyterian Church in the United States of America....................	418	398	3,285,860	8,256	103	263,743
44	Colored Cumberland Presbyterian Church	164	162	353,825	2,184	35	25,095
45	United Presbyterian Church of North America....................	13	12	189,300	15,775	....	....
46	Presbyterian Church in the United States.	47	46	138,140	3,003	10	2,102
47	Protestant Episcopal Church............	263	259	4,162,735	16,072	50	284,374
48	Reformed Episcopal Church.............	36	36	59,850	1,663	8	2,694
49	Roman Catholic Church................	129	126	4,667,378	37,043	43	851,461
50	Salvation Army......................	1	1	67,064	....	1	21,400
	Spiritualists:						
51	Progressive Spiritual Church..........	1	1	3,800	....	....	....

[1] This and the following tables are from the *Census of Religious*

244

SEPARATE FIGURES FOR URBAN AND RURAL CHURCHES, BY DENOMINATIONS.—*Cont.*

in 1920, the date of the last Federal Census, rural territory comprises the remainder of the country]

	URBAN CHURCHES						RURAL CHURCHES					
Number of church edifices	Value of church edifices			Debt on church edifices		Number of church edifices	Value of church edifices			Debt on church edifices		
	Churches reporting	Amount (dollars)	Average per church (dollars)	Churches reporting	Amount (dollars)		Churches reporting	Amount (dollars)	Average per church (dollars)	Churches reporting	Amount (dollars)	
9	9	67,300	7,478	1	3,600	13	13	15,800	1,215	......	550,218	32
1,446	1,424	23,994,224	16,850	728	2,782,754	4,481	4,405	8,098,325	1,838	1,180	550,218	33
615	615	13,451,618	21,873	245	1,602,747	1,755	1,755	5,064,105	2,886	369	234,605	34
3	3	36,000	12,000	1	1,200	......	......	......	......	......	......	35
33	32	380,150	11,880	15	39,464	32	32	98,801	3,088	8	2,830	36
21	20	381,483	19,074	14	20,675	22	20	94,786	4,729	3	1,250	37
524	521	5,791,115	11,115	229	821,462	1,822	1,820	3,420,322	1,879	362	138,662	38
3	3	57,000	19,000	3	9,000	43	42	127,075	3,026	14	2,681	39
9	4	29,450	7,363	2	2,800	19	17	45,350	2,668	3	910	40
8	7	74,000	10,571	6	31,297	21	21	24,050	1,145	8	4,322	41
1	1	30,000	......	......	......	......	......	......	......	......	......	42
186	171	2,718,550	15,898	61	243,029	232	227	567,310	2,499	42	20,714	43
54	52	167,920	3,229	20	20,710	110	110	185,905	1,690	15	4,385	44
7	6	126,000	21,000	......	......	6	6	63,300	10,550	......	......	45
16	15	92,175	6,145	4	1,670	31	31	45,965	1,483	6	432	46
192	188	3,958,210	21,054	45	281,321	71	71	204,525	2,881	5	3,053	47
7	7	29,500	4,214	3	753	29	29	30,350	1,047	5	1,941	48
104	101	4,484,128	44,397	41	843,711	25	25	183,250	7,330	2	7,750	49
1	1	67,064	......	1	21,400	......	......	......	......	......	......	50
1	1	3,800	......	......	......	......	......	......	......	......	......	51

Bodies of the United States Bureau of the Census, taken in 1926.

	DENOMINATION	Total number of churches[1] in denominations wholly or in part Negro	NUMBER OF NEGRO CHURCHES[1]		
			Total	Urban	Rural
	All denominations.....................	**141,753**	**42,585**	**10,158**	**32,427**
1	Adventist bodies:				
2	Advent Christian Church......................	444	6	1	5
3	Seventh-day Adventist Denomination............	1,981	93	88	5
4	African Orthodox Church......................	13	13	13	....
5	African Orthodox Church of New York	3	3	3	....
6	Apostolic Overcoming Holy Church of God..........	16	16	8	8
	Baptist bodies:				
7	Negro Baptists......................	22,081	22,081	4,409	17,672
8	United American Free Will Baptist Church	166	166	11	155
9	Regular Baptists......................	349	1	....	1
10	Colored Primitive Baptists.....................	925	925	76	849
11	Christian and Missionary Alliance.................	332	10	9	1
12	Christian Church (General Convention of the Christian Church).........................	1,044	68	18	50
13	Church of Christ (Holiness), U.S.A................	82	82	46	36
14	Church of Christ, Scientist.......................	1,913	1	1	....
15	Church of God........................	644	29	7	22
16	Church of God (headquarters, Anderson, Ind.).......	932	98	54	44
17	Church of God and Saints of Christ...............	112	112	101	11
18	Church of God in Christ.........................	733	733	405	328
19	Churches of Christ.........................	6,226	214	80	134
20	Churches of God, Holiness......................	29	29	24	5
21	Churches of God in North America (General Eldership)	428	7	2	5
	Churches of the Living God:				
22	Church of the Living God, Christian Workers for Fellowship.........................	149	149	82	67
23	Church of the Living God, "The Pillar and Ground of Truth".................................	81	81	45	36
24	Congregational Churches.........................	5,028	155	96	59
25	Disciples of Christ.............................	7,648	487	160	327
26	Free Christian Zion Church of Christ..............	5	5	1	4
27	Free Church of God in Christ....................	19	19	15	4
28	Independent churches...........................	259	7	7	....
	Lutheran bodies:				
29	United Lutheran Church in America.............	3,650	1	1	....
	Evangelical Lutheran Synodical Conference of America—				
30	Evangelical Lutheran Synod of Missouri, Ohio, and Other States...............................	3,917	69	33	36
	Methodist bodies:				
31	Methodist Episcopal Church....................	26,130	3,743	805	2,938
32	Methodist Protestant Church....................	2,239	46	9	37
33	Wesleyan Methodist Connection (or Church) of America......................................	619	26	10	16
34	African Methodist Episcopal Church.............	6,708	6,708	1,599	5,109
35	African Methodist Episcopal Zion Church.........	2,466	2,466	650	1,816
36	Colored Methodist Protestant Church.............	3	3	3	....

[1] Includes only organizations reporting members.
[2] Membership as defined by the particular denomination.

NUMBERS OF MEMBERS[2]			AVERAGE MEMBERS PER CHURCH			TOTAL MEMBERSHIP BY SEX[3]				
Total	Urban	Rural	Total	Urban	Rural	Male	Female	Sex not reported	Males per 100 females	
5,203,487	2,238,871	2,964,616	122	220	91	1,726,347	2,789,749	687,391	61.9	
										1
164	22	142	27	.....	28	83	81	....	(4)	2
5,133	5,052	81	55	57	16	1,272	3,831	30	33.2	3
1,568	1,568	....	121	121	....	689	879	....	78.4	4
717	717	....	239	239	....	262	355	100	73.8	5
1,047	581	466	65	73	58	352	695	....	50.6	6
3,196,623	1,246,327	1,950,296	145	283	110	1,050,062	1,661,183	485,378	63.2	7
13,396	1,804	11,592	81	164	75	5,079	8,236	81	61.7	8
38	....	38	.....	.....	....	16	22	....	(4)	9
43,978	4,637	39,341	48	61	46	2,346	4,856	36,776	48.3	10
535	510	25	54	57	....	198	337	....	58.8	11
7,312	1,705	5,607	108	95	112	2,690	4,622	....	58.2	12
4,919	3,002	1,917	60	65	53	1,589	2,942	388	54.0	13
274	274	....	.....	.....	....	70	204	....	34.3	14
887	318	569	31	45	26	296	591	....	50.1	15
3,165	2,404	761	32	45	17	1,072	2,093	....	51.2	16
6,741	6,055	686	60	60	62	2,539	4,202	....	60.4	17
30,263	20,805	9,458	41	51	29	9,077	20,873	313	43.5	18
8,155	3,580	4,575	38	45	34	3,296	4,839	20	68.1	19
2,278	1,929	349	79	80	70	830	1,410	38	58.9	20
274	55	219	39	28	44	103	171	....	60.2	21
11,558	7,289	4,269	78	89	64	3,964	7,594	....	52.2	22
5,844	3,886	1,958	72	86	54	3,247	2,597	....	125.0	23
16,000	13,139	2,861	103	137	48	6,081	9,782	137	62.2	24
37,325	14,938	22,387	77	93	68	12,016	18,459	6,850	65.1	25
187	60	127	37	.....	32	94	93	....	(4)	26
874	797	77	46	53	19	300	574	....	52.3	27
1,542	1,542	....	220	220	....	401	1,021	120	39.3	28
126	126	....	.....	.....	....	73	53	....	(4)	29
5,871	3,596	2,275	85	109	63	2,480	3,308	83	75.0	30
332,347	149,559	182,788	89	186	62	117,176	192,905	22,266	60.7	31
2,529	305	2,224	55	34	60	725	1,164	640	62.3	32
1,215	672	543	47	67	34	424	791	....	53.6	33
545,814	272,765	273,049	81	171	53	165,615	295,137	85,062	56.1	34
456,813	193,926	262,887	185	298	145	167,432	289,381	....	57.9	35
533	533	....	178	178	....	194	339	....	57.2	36

[3] Figures are to be used with due consideration of the number of members not so reported.
[4] Ratio not shown where number of females is less than 100.

	DENOMINATION	Total number of churches[1] in denominations wholly or in part Negro	NUMBER OF NEGRO CHURCHES[1]		
			Total	Urban	Rural
37	Union American Methodist Episcopal Church......	73	73	37	36
38	African Union Methodist Protestant Church......	43	43	23	20
39	Colored Methodist Episcopal Church...........	2,518	2,518	567	1,951
40	Reformed Zion Union Apostolic Church.........	48	48	5	43
41	Reformed Methodist Union Episcopal Church.....	25	25	7	18
42	Independent African Methodist Episcopal Church..	29	29	8	21
	Moravian bodies:				
43	Moravian Church in America..................	127	1	1	....
44	The (Original) Church of God	50	1	1	....
	Presbyterian bodies:				
45	Presbyterian Church in the United States of America	8,947	450	195	255
46	Colored Cumberland Presbyterian Church........	178	178	60	118
47	United Presbyterian Church of North America....	901	14	6	8
48	Presbyterian Church in the United States........	3,469	52	17	35
49	Protestant Episcopal Church.....................	7,299	287	205	82
50	Reformed Episcopal Church......................	69	36	7	29
51	Roman Catholic Church.........................	18,940	147	117	30
52	Salvation Army.................................	1,052	5	5	....
	Spiritualists:				
53	National Spiritualist Association................	543	17	17	....
54	Progressive Spiritual Church....................	9	1	1	....
55	National Spiritual Alliance of the United States of America...................................	59	8	7	1

NUMBERS OF MEMBERS[2]			AVERAGE MEMBERS PER CHURCH			TOTAL MEMBERSHIP BY SEX[2]				
Total	Urban	Rural	Total	Urban	Rural	Male	Female	Sex not reported	Males per 100 females	
10,169	7,043	3,126	139	190	87	4,223	5,946	....	71.0	37
4,086	2,707	1,379	95	118	69	1,255	1,786	1,045	70.3	38
202,713	79,183	123,530	81	140	63	65,781	107,807	29,125	61.0	39
4,538	651	3,887	95	130	90	1,876	2,544	118	73.7	40
2,265	486	1,779	91	69	99	764	1,501	....	50.9	41
1,003	424	579	35	53	28	351	652	....	53.8	42
694	694	....	.....	.....	.....	250	444	....	56.3	43
12	12	....	.....	.....	.....	....	....	12	......	44
37,090	21,503	15,587	82	110	61	14,048	21,376	1,666	65.7	45
10,868	3,911	6,957	61	65	59	4,410	6,373	85	69.2	46
1,202	602	600	86	100	75	421	668	113	63.0	47
2,134	907	1,227	41	53	35	817	1,303	14	62.7	48
51,502	46,201	5,301	179	225	65	17,846	26,422	7,234	67.5	49
2,753	1,158	1,595	76	165	55	926	1,827	....	50.7	50
124,324	106,839	17,485	846	913	583	50,732	64,523	9,069	78.6	51
495	495	....	99	99	.....	140	355	....	39.4	52
904	904	....	53	53	.....	100	176	628	56.8	53
500	500	....	.....	.....	.....	200	300	....	66.7	54
190	173	17	24	25	.....	64	126	....	50.8	55

	DENOMINATION	Total number of churches	VALUE OF PARSONAGES			DEBT ON PARSONAGES	
			Churches reporting	Amount (dollars)	Average per church (dollars)	Churches reporting	Amount (dollars)
1	All denominations...............	42,585	6,543	18,122,240	2,770	1,399	1,824,255
	Adventist bodies:						
2	Advent Christian Church..............	6	......	......	......	......	......
3	Seventh-day Advent Denomination......	93	6	27,200	4,533	2	5,700
4	African Orthodox Church..............	13	1	5,000	....	1	2,000
5	African Orthodox Church of New York....	3	1	15,000	....	1	11,000
6	Apostolic Overcoming Holy Church of God.	16	1	3,000	....	......	......
	Baptist bodies:						
7	Negro Baptists......................	22,081	1,325	4,451,057	3,359	376	634,369
8	United American Free Will Baptist Church..........................	166	2	1,300	650	1	40
9	Regular Baptists....................	1	......	......	......	......	......
10	Colored Primitive Baptists.............	925	......	......	......	......	......
11	Christian and Missionary Alliance........	10	1	1,875	....	1	1,250
12	Christian Church (General Convention of the Christian Church).................	68	1	5,000	....	......	......
13	Church of Christ, Holiness................	82	11	30,500	2,773	6	4,222
14	Church of Christ, Scientist...............	1	......	......	......	......	......
15	Church of God......................	29	2	6,000	3,000	......	......
16	Church of God (headquarters, Anderson, Ind.).................................	98	9	60,200	6,689	2	13,700
17	Church of God and Saints of Christ........	112	23	68,450	2,976	9	17,439
18	Church of God in Christ..................	733	48	85,000	1,771	25	22,941
19	Churches of Christ....................	214	......	......	......	......	......
20	Churches of God Holiness..............	29	2	16,700	8,350	1	10,000
21	Churches of God in North America (General Eldership)........................	7	......	......	......	......	......
	Churches of the Living God:						
22	Church of the Living God,"The Pillar and Ground of Truth"..................	81	14	25,100	1,793	2	3,350
23	Church of the Living God, Christian Workers for Fellowship..............	149	4	6,300	1,575	2	1,700
24	Congregational Churches.................	155	59	262,150	4,443	22	49,827
25	Disciples of Christ......................	487	30	93,300	3,110	8	16,600
26	Free Christian Zion Church of Christ.......	5	......	......	......	......	......
27	Free Church of God in Christ..............	19	1	2,000	....	1	1,000
28	Independent Churches...................	7	......	......	......	......	......
	Lutheran bodies:						
29	United Lutheran Church of America......	1	......	......	......	......	......
30	Evangelical Lutheran Synodical Conference of America— Evangelical Lutheran Synod of Missouri, Ohio and Other States........	69	13	20,700	1,592	......	......
	Methodist bodies:						
31	Methodist Episcopal Church............	3,743	1,419	2,922,791	2,060	312	282,053
32	Methodist Protestant Church...........	46	3	2,100	700	1	700

[1]The statistics given relate only to the Sunday schools reported by individual churches and do not include undenominational or union Sunday schools; nor do they include the parochial or week-day schools that are maintained.

AND STATISTICS OF SUNDAY SCHOOLS, DISTINGUISHED AS URBAN AND RURAL,
ATIONS: 1926

in 1920, the date of the last Federal census; rural territory comprises the remainder of the country]

ALL SUNDAY SCHOOLS [1]				URBAN SUNDAY SCHOOLS [1]				RURAL SUNDAY SCHOOLS [1]				
Chrches reporting	Officers and teachers	Scholars	Average scholars per church	Churches reporting	Officers and teachers	Scholars	Average scholars per church	Churches reporting	Officers and teachers	Scholars	Average scholars per church	
36,378	298,283	2,144,553	59	9,028	100,486	866,068	96	27,350	197,797	1,278,485	47	1
4	20	94	24	1	4	15	....	3	16	79	26	2
67	575	3,402	51	63	557	3,321	53	4	18	81	20	3
11	49	445	40	11	49	445	40	......	......	......	......	4
3	26	220	73	3	26	220	73	......	......	......	......	5
15	67	1,068	71	7	38	583	83	8	29	485	61	6
18,755	148,067	1,121,362	60	3,918	45,039	402,416	103	14,837	103,028	718,946	48	7
144	836	5,077	35	11	80	709	64	133	756	4,368	33	8
......	......	......	......	......	......	......	......	......	......	......	......	9
24	179	2,278	95	10	70	780	78	14	109	1,498	107	10
8	57	490	61	7	54	465	66	1	3	25	....	11
64	433	3,348	52	16	123	955	60	48	310	2,393	50	12
72	460	2,511	35	40	249	1,482	37	32	211	1,029	32	13
1	72	395	......	1	72	395	......	......	......	......	......	14
24	138	901	38	7	40	246	35	17	98	655	39	15
89	499	3,131	35	52	350	2,296	44	37	149	835	23	16
67	303	2,010	30	60	262	1,751	29	7	41	259	37	17
585	3,216	19,282	33	331	2,011	12,666	38	254	1,205	6,616	26	18
177	505	5,905	33	71	233	2,819	40	106	272	3,086	29	19
27	174	1,246	46	22	148	1,066	48	5	26	180	36	20
7	33	298	43	2	13	109	55	5	20	189	38	21
26	169	1,468	56	19	132	1,177	62	7	37	291	42	22
140	444	3,465	25	77	285	2,171	28	63	159	1,294	21	23
140	1,082	8,899	64	86	815	6,862	80	54	267	2,037	38	24
397	2,081	14,848	37	133	876	6,179	46	264	1,205	8,669	33	25
5	22	97	19	1	5	35	....	4	17	62	16	26
17	100	633	37	14	87	568	41	3	13	65	22	27
6	45	491	82	6	45	491	82	......	......	......	......	28
1	8	90	....	1	8	90	....	......	......	......	......	29
61	210	3,314	54	26	107	1,801	69	35	103	1,513	43	30
3,527	25,846	196,496	56	778	8,712	83,357	107	2,749	17,134	113,139	41	31
42	207	1,283	31	8	34	203	25	34	173	1,080	32	32

by a number of bodies, particularly the Roman Catholic Church, and certain Lutheran bodies. Information regarding the various types of religious instruction is given elsewhere.

251

TABLE XVIII. — NEGRO CHURCHES — VALUE OF PARSONAGES AND DEBT, BY DENOMINATIONS:

[Urban territory includes all cities and other incorporated places which had 2,500 inhabitants or more

	DENOMINATION	Total number of churches	VALUE OF PARSONAGES			DEBT ON PARSONAGES	
			Churches reporting	Amount (dollars)	Average per church (dollars)	Churches reporting	Amount (dollars)
33	Wesleyan Methodist Connection (or Church) of America.................	26	4	4,600	1,150	......	....
34	African Methodist Episcopal Church.....	6,708	2,134	4,857,996	2,276	354	357,137
35	African Methodist Episcopal Zion Church.	2,466	478	1,916,950	4,010	72	111,973
36	Colored Methodist Protestant Church....	3	......	....	....	......	....
37	Union American Methodist Episcopal. Church...........................	73	15	57,100	3,807	11	14,144
38	African Union Methodist Protestant Church.........................	43	15	44,050	2,937	3	3,273
39	Colored Methodist Episcopal Church.....	2,518	530	984,660	1,858	109	93,929
40	Reformed Zion Union Apostolic Church...	48	1	500	500	1	200
41	Reformed Methodist Union Episcopal Church...........................	25	6	7,500	1,250	......	....
42	Independent African Methodist Episcopal Church...........................	29	3	7,500	2,500	2	1,750
	Moravian bodies:						
43	Moravian Church in America...........	1	1	10,000	....	......	....
44	The (Original) Church of God.............	1	......	....	....	......	....
	Presbyterian bodies:						
45	Presbyterian Church in the United States of America.....................	450	137	539,455	3,938	34	35,236
46	Colored Cumberland Presbyterian Church.	178	10	9,700	970	2	450
47	United Presbyterian Church of North America.....................	14	5	22,300	4,460	......	....
48	Presbyterian Church in the United States..	52	15	31,850	2,123	4	6,900
49	Protestant Episcopal Church.............	287	116	636,250	5,485	19	58,225
50	Reformed Episcopal Church.............	36	1	1,200	....	......	....
51	Roman Catholic Church.................	147	96	879,906	9,166	15	63,147
52	Salvation Army.......................	5	......	....	....	......	....
	Spiritualists:						
53	National Spiritualist Association.........	17	......	....	....	......	....
54	Progressive Spiritual Church...........	1	......	....	....	......	....
55	National Spiritual Alliance of the United States of America...................	8	......	....	....	......	....

in 1920, the date of the last Federal Census, rural territory comprises the remainder of the country]

ALL SUNDAY SCHOOLS [1]				URBAN SUNDAY SCHOOLS [1]				RURAL SUNDAY SCHOOLS [1]				
Churches reporting	Officers and teachers	Scholars	Average scholars per church	Churches reporting	Officers and teachers	Scholar	Average scholars per church	Churches reporting	Officers and teachers	Scholars	Average scholars per church	
26	196	1,084	42	10	96	578	58	16	100	506	32	33
5,884	43,383	288,247	49	1,454	16,544	139,608	96	4,430	26,839	148,639	34	34
2,429	45,087	267,141	110	640	14,200	103,542	162	1,789	30,887	163,599	91	35
3	18	98	33	3	18	98	33	......	......	......	......	36
69	428	4,240	61	37	268	3,019	82	32	160	1,221	38	37
42	273	2,851	68	22	142	1,724	78	20	131	1,127	56	38
2,351	15,666	103,523	44	540	4,413	34,571	64	1,811	11,253	68,952	38	39
42	325	2,882	69	5	37	394	79	37	288	2,488	67	40
19	107	673	35	3	21	78	26	16	86	595	37	41
26	141	663	26	8	44	280	35	18	97	383	21	42
1	21	208	......	1	21	208	......	......	......	......	......	43
......	......	......	......	......	......	......	......	......	......	......	......	44
400	3,137	27,817	70	181	1,727	15,598	86	219	1,410	12,219	56	45
152	840	5,223	34	51	295	1,763	35	101	545	3,460	34	46
14	126	1,587	113	6	64	764	127	8	62	823	103	47
13	231	1,569	36	16	98	777	49	27	133	792	29	48
260	1,717	19,075	73	190	1,450	15,704	83	70	267	3,371	48	49
28	160	1,216	43	7	48	450	64	21	112	766	36	50
76	462	11,400	150	65	434	10,736	165	11	28	670	61	51
5	39	470	94	5	39	470	94	......	......	......	......	52
1	1	10	......	1	1	10	......	......	......	......	......	53
......	......	......	......	......	......	......	......	......	......	......	......	54
1	2	23	......	1	2	23	......	......	......	......	......	55

TABLE XIX.—NEGRO CHURCHES—CHURCH EXPENDITURES DURING YEAR, WITH

[Urban territory includes all cities and other incorporated places which had 2,500 inhabitants or more

	DENOMINATION	Churches reporting	Total expenditures (dollars)	For current expenses and improvements (dollars)	For benevolences, missions, etc. (dollars)	Not classified (dollars)	Average Per church (dollars
		ALL CHURCHES					
1	All denominations.........	39,245	43,024,259	35,749,951	6,152,905	1,121,403	1,096
2	Adventist bodies: Advent Christian Church.......	4	240	25	215	....	60
3	Seventh-day Adventist Denomination.......................	85	261,975	94,525	167,450	....	3,082
4	African Orthodox Church..........	13	19,368	18,211	1,157	....	1,490
5	African Orthodox Church of NewYork	2	18,900	15,200	3,700	....	9,450
6	Apostolic Over-coming Holy Church of God........................	16	17,198	15,010	2,188	....	1,075
7	Baptist bodies: Negro Baptists.................	20,209	19,475,981	16,210,952	2,444,042	820,987	964
8	United American Free Will Baptist Church...................	158	67,773	46,494	13,090	8,189	429
9	Colored Primitive Baptists........	111	39,419	26,874	12,052	493	355
10	Christian and Missionary Alliance....	10	19,177	12,907	6,270	....	1,918
11	Christian Church (General Convention of the Christian Church)......	68	45,739	38,267	7,038	434	673
12	Church of Christ, Holiness..........	64	48,968	36,532	8,191	4,245	765
13	Church of Christ, Scientist..........	1	38,995	32,397	6,598	....	....
14	Church of God....................	25	39,064	34,555	3,909	600	1,563
15	Church of God (headquarters, Anderson, Ind.).................	82	86,094	75,573	9,030	1,491	1,050
16	Church of God and Saints of Christ...	100	137,345	76,414	53,917	7,014	1,373
17	Church of God in Christ............	624	516,011	394,773	90,384	30,854	827
18	Churches of Christ................	212	40,996	34,886	5,595	515	193
19	Churches of God, Holiness	26	35,878	27,878	8,000	....	1,380
20	Churches of God in North America (General Eldership).............	7	2,380	2,066	249	65	340
21	Churches of the Living God: Church of the Living God, Christian Workers of Fellowship......	144	50,515	45,989	4,526	....	351
22	Church of the Living God, "The Pillar and Ground of Truth"	81	64,555	51,284	13,271	....	797
23	Congregational Churches..........	144	316,444	295,446	20,388	610	2,198
24	Disciples of Christ................	447	289,721	239,279	33,125	17,317	648
25	Free Christian Zion Church of Christ	5	2,481	2,006	475	....	496
26	Free Church of God in Christ........	18	19,540	12,505	7,035	....	1,086
27	Independent churches..............	6	34,904	32,044	2,860	....	5,817
28	Lutheran bodies: United Lutheran Church in America	1	306	211	95	....	....
29	Evangelical Lutheran Synodical Conference of America— Evangelical Lutheran Synod of Missouri, Ohio, and Other States....................	67	72,197	62,421	7,096	2,680	1,078
30	Methodist bodies: Methodist Episcopal Church......	3,682	3,694,508	3,138,411	550,561	5,536	1,003
31	Methodist Protestant Church	44	11,495	8,946	2,299	250	261

Separate Figures for Urban and Rural Churches, by Denominations: 1926

in 1920, the date of the last Federal census, rural territory comprises the remainder of the country]

	URBAN CHURCHES					RURAL CHURCHES				
Churches reporting	Total expenditures (including not classified) (dollars)	For current expenses and improvements (dollars)	For benevolences, missions, etc. (dollars)	Average per church (dollars)	Churches reporting	Total expenditures (including not classified) (dollars)	For current expenses and improvements (dollars)	For benevolences, missions, etc. (dollars)	Average per church (dollars)	
9,642	26,402,536	22,292,954	3,455,369	2,738	29,603	16,621,723	13,456,997	2,697,536	561	1
1	100	....	100	....	3	140	25	115	47	2
80	260,938	94,294	166,644	3,262	5	1,037	231	806	207	3
13	19,368	18,211	1,157	1,490	......	....	....	....	......	4
2	18,900	15,200	3,700	9,450	......	....	....	....	......	5
8	11,187	9,935	1,252	1,398	8	6,011	5,075	936	751	6
4,186	11,553,870	9,804,889	1,265,608	2,760	16,023	7,922,111	6,406,063	1,178,434	494	7
11	12,975	10,056	1,467	1,180	147	54,798	36,438	11,623	373	8
30	19,362	13,630	5,389	645	81	20,057	13,244	6,663	248	9
9	18,977	12,707	6,270	2,109	1	200	200	....	......	10
18	23,465	21,253	1,778	1,304	50	22,274	17,014	5,260	445	11
33	36,006	27,776	4,718	1,091	31	12,962	8,756	3,473	418	12
1	38,995	32,397	6,598	......	......	....	....	....	......	13
6	21,644	19,750	1,894	3,607	19	17,420	14,805	2,015	917	14
46	77,258	68,591	7,206	1,680	36	8,836	6,982	1,824	245	15
91	129,220	72,297	52,716	1,420	9	8,125	4,117	1,201	903	16
359	417,906	322,234	70,874	1,164	265	98,105	72,539	19,510	370	17
80	26,373	22,069	4,304	330	132	14,623	12,817	1,291	111	18
21	34,693	26,769	7,924	1,652	5	1,185	1,109	76	237	19
2	1,309	1,428	116	805	5	771	638	133	154	20
80	36,626	33,164	3,462	458	64	13,889	12,825	1,064	217	21
45	43,338	32,682	10,656	963	36	21,217	18,602	2,615	589	22
91	276,793	258,576	17,607	3,042	53	39,651	36,870	2,781	748	23
145	189,315	165,795	17,524	1,306	302	100,406	73,484	15,601	332	24
1	1,806	1,506	300	......	4	675	500	175	169	25
15	16,440	10,805	5,635	1,096	3	3,100	1,700	1,400	1,033	26
6	34,904	32,044	2,860	5,817	......	....	....	....	......	27
1	306	211	95	......	......	....	....	....	......	28
32	54,634	48,081	5,417	1,707	35	17,563	14,340	1,679	502	29
793	2,112,660	1,797,791	314,869	2,664	2,889	1,581,848	1,340,620	235,692	548	30
9	2,772	2,370	402	308	35	8,723	6,576	1,897	249	31

	DENOMINATION	Churches reporting	Total expenditures (dollars)	For current expenses and improvements (dollars)	For benevolences, missions,etc (dollars)	Not classified (dollars)	Average per church (dollars)
				ALL CHURCHES			
32	Wesleyan Methodist Connection (or Church) of America.........	25	16,679	13,781	2,898	....	667
33	African Methodist Episcopal Church	6,492	7,600,161	6,205,632	1,257,397	137,132	1,171
34	African Methodist Episcopal Zion Church......................	2,464	4,757,066	4,091,023	662,993	3,050	1,931
35	Colored Methodist Protestant Church....................	3	6,685	5,660	1,025	....	2,228
36	Union American Methodist Episcipal Church................	68	222,621	202,075	20,546	....	3,274
37	African Union Methodist Protestant Church.................	43	99,563	88,272	11,291	....	2,315
38	Colored Methodist Episcopal Church....................	2,477	2,428,234	1,934,540	417,038	76,656	980
39	Reformed Zion Union Apostolic Church....................	44	37,601	24,627	13,334	....	855
40	Reformed Methodist Union Episcopal Church................	24	17,282	14,744	2,538	....	720
41	Independent African Methodist Episcopal Church.............	27	11,704	9,958	1,746	....	433
	Moravian bodies:						
42	Moravian Church in America......	1	4,475	3,555	920	....	.....
	Presbyterian bodies:						
43	Presbyterian Church in the United States of America.............	438	604,179	536,923	66,356	900	1,379
44	Colored Cumberland Presbyterian Church....................	167	80,304	70,437	9,867	....	481
45	United Presbyterian Church of North America...............	12	20,211	14,043	6,168	....	1,684
46	Presbyterian Church in the United States......................	51	27,846	22,005	5,826	15	546
47	Protestant Episcopal Church........	272	572,108	483,912	87,826	370	2,103
48	Reformed Episcopal Church.......	35	18,417	12,470	5,947	....	526
49	Roman Catholic Church............	129	1,005,645	913,914	89,731	2,000	7,796
50	Salvation Army..................	5	15,118	12,345	2,773	....	3,024
	Spiritualists:						
51	National Spiritualist Association...	9	7,655	6,114	1,541	....	851
52	Progressive Spiritual Church......	1	2,125	2,000	125	....	.....
53	National Spiritual Alliance of the United States of America.......	2	413	200	213	....	207

in 1920, the date of the last Federal Census, rural territory comprises the remainder of the country.]

	URBAN CHURCHES					RURAL CHURCHES				
Churches reporting	Total expenditures (including not classified) (dollars)	For current expenses and improvements (dollars)	For benevolences, missions, etc. (dollars)	Average per church (dollars)	Churches reporting	Total expenditures (including not classified) (dollars)	For current expenses and improvements (dollars)	For benevolences, missions, etc. (dollars)	Average per church (dollars)	
10	11,777	10,422	1,355	1,178	15	4,902	3,359	1,543	327	32
1,532	4,803,582	3,993,308	726,635	3,135	4,960	2,796,579	2,212,324	530,762	564	33
649	2,576,570	2,284,192	292,378	3,970	1,815	2,180,496	1,806,831	370,615	1,201	34
3	6,685	5,660	1,025	2,228	......	....	....	....	......	35
35	159,514	145,485	14,029	4,558	33	63,107	56,590	6,517	1,912	36
23	64,186	56,738	7,448	2,791	20	35,377	31,534	3,843	1,769	37
558	1,191,659	962,220	189,414	2,136	1,919	1,236,575	972,320	227,624	644	38
5	10,292	7,264	3,028	2,058	39	27,309	17,003	10,306	700	39
6	7,064	6,255	809	1,177	18	10,218	8,289	1,729	568	40
8	7,837	7,374	463	980	19	3,867	2,584	1,283	204	41
0	4,475	3,555	920	......	......	....	....	....	......	42
192	468,451	425,149	42,402	2,440	246	135,728	111,774	23,954	552	43
56	38,569	34,049	4,520	689	111	41,735	36,388	5,347	376	44
5	10,167	7,692	2,475	2,033	7	10,044	6,351	3,693	1,435	45
17	18,771	14,287	4,484	1,104	34	9,075	7,718	1,342	267	46
198	547,923	465,947	81,714	2,767	74	24,185	17,965	6,112	327	47
7	10,794	7,197	3,597	1,542	28	7,623	5,273	2,350	272	48
105	946,469	858,990	85,479	9,014	24	59,176	54,924	4,252	2,466	49
5	15,118	12,345	2,773	3,024	......	....	....	....	......	50
9	7,655	6,114	1,541	851	......	....	....	....	......	51
1	2,125	2,000	125	......	......	....	....	....	......	52
2	413	200	213	207	......	....	....	....	......	53

INDEX

A

Abila, a settlement, 117
Agriculture, the employment of the majority of Negroes in, 88
Alabama, peonage in, 68, 69, 70, 71, 72, 73, 81, 88; turpentine industry in, 100; wood distillation in, 101; fisheries of, 103; mining and quarrying in, 104; rural schools in, 208, 209, 210, 212, 217, 220; Negro voters in, 240-241
Allensworth, a settlement, 117
Amusements in the rural communities, 132-149
Andy, a Negro settlement, 119
Archery, a settlement, 119
Arkansas, peonage in, 77-78; riot in, 84-85; mining and quarrying in, 104; a Negro settlement in, 117; rural schools in, 209, 211
Attendance at school, the early, 185-187, 203-221
Automobile, the rise of, in rural communities, 141
Averett, a settlement in Virginia, 116

B

Bailey vs. *State of Alabama*, peonage question involved in, 70-71
Baldwin Farms, a settlement, 116
Baptist churches, statistics of, 153; and tables in Appendix
Barret, a settlement, 115
Bible teaching in rural communities, 166-170
Biscoe, a settlement, 119
Boley, a Negro settlement in Oklahoma, 119, 121

Bond, Scott, of Arkansas, 111
Bookertee, a settlement, 119
Bowles, a settlement, 117
Brickmaking, statistics of, 95, 96, 97
Brooklyn, a settlement in Illinois, 117, 121
Brownlee, a settlement, 115-116
Building rural churches, 174-175
Burroughs, a settlement, 119
Business man, the handicaps of, in the country, 65
Buxton, a Negro mining town, 121

C

Cabin Creek, a settlement, 115
Callas, Joseph, a Russian Jew, held as a peon, 77-78
Calloway, C. J., work of; in the rural school, 195; a voter, 240
Calvin Township settlement, 115
Camp Nelson, a Negro settlement, 120
Canning, statistics of, 95, 96, 97, 101-102
Cannonville, a settlement, 119
Caucasian, the leadership of, 227-228
Cary, Mississippi, experience of Negro agent in wreck at, 234-235
Cedarlake, a community, 119
Chambers, a settlement, 117
Charleston, immigrants to, 79
Chesapeake and Ohio Railway, the attitude of a hospital of, 14-15
Church, the rural, 150-178; attitude of, toward amusements, 132, 133, 136, 139, 140, 144-145, 146; statistics of, 150, 153, 172-173, and tables in the Appendix

259

Ohio, industry in, 105
Oklahoma, industry in, 104; rural schools in, 205, 212, 219, 220; Negro voters in, 240
Overchurching in the rural community, 176
Owen, Mrs. of Alabama, statement of, 239

P

Pace, J. W., a peonist, 78
Peace, a Negro settlement, 117
Peasant proprietorship, the advocacy of, 55-59
Peasants, Negro, the health of, 1-21
"Peonage" 23, 67-88, 92; quotations respecting, 75, 76; cases, 75, 76, 77, 78; in New Jersey, 82-83
Peonists, the words of, in their own defense, 79-80
"Personality of law" in rural communities, 231-232
Pennsylvania, industry in, 105
Physical education, the lack of, in the country, 9, 10
Physicians, Negro, the lack of, 16, 18; prejudice against, 16
Place, the Negro's, 229, 230, 231, 232
Plantations, break-up of, 34, 35
Planter class, attitude of, toward amusements for Negroes, 22-88, 134, 135; attitude of, toward ministers, 176-177
Plateau, a settlement, 119, 122, 123
Poles, Russian, held as peons 78
Porter, a settlement, 119
Poverty, 139
Preacher, the handicaps of, 64-65
Preserving, statistics of, 95, 96, 97
Pringle, Hezzie, deliverance of a peon by, 86
Program, lack of in the rural Negro church, 151, 152, 153, 154, 166-170
Prostitution in the country, 7-8
Public schools, the early, 183

Q

Quarrying, statistics of, 95-96; 104-105

R

Race prejudice, a handicap to the interdenominational church, 178-179
Racial antagonism, 24
Randolph settlement, the, 115
Recreation in rural communities, 132-149
Red Cross, attitude of, toward peons, 86-88
Redbird, a settlement, 119
Religion, neglect of, 63-64, 65
Religious caste, 227, 228, 229
Religious practices, 151, 152, 154, 159, 164, 165
Religious education, the lack of in rural communities, 166-170, 177-178
Renova, a settlement, 119
Rentiesville, a settlement, 119
Results of the rural school development, 199-202
Revolution in agriculture, 44; in amusements and recreation, 138, 139, 140
Robbins, a settlement, 117
Roberts, a settlement, 115, 119
Rosenwald, Julius, interest of, in rural schools, 193; quotations from, 193
Rosenwald Schools, 180-224
Rural communities, health in, 1-21; other data on, 110-131
Rural physicians, lack of training of, 18; antiquated methods of, 18
Rural Schools, 180-224

S

Salaries of rural clergy, 174
School attendance, 203-221
School enrollment, 203-221
Schoolhouses, the lack of, 184-185
Sectarian bias a handicap, 176, 178-179; diminished by rural school development, 199